Literary Tourism

Jasna Potočnik Topler

Literary Tourism
The Case of Norman Mailer
Mailer's Life and Legacy

Bibliographic Information published by the Deutsche Nationalbibliothek
The Deutsche Nationalbibliothek lists this publication in
the Deutsche Nationalbibliografie; detailed bibliographic
data is available in the internet at http://dnb.d-nb.de.

Library of Congress Cataloging-in-Publication Data
Potocnik Topler, Jasna.
  Literary tourism : the case of Norman Mailer: Mailer's life and legacy / Jasna Potocnik Topler.
      pages cm
  Includes bibliographical references and index.
  ISBN 978-3-631-67018-7
  1. Mailer, Norman--Criticism and interpretation. 2. Mailer, Norman--Homes and haunts. 3. Literature and society--United States--History--20th century. 4. Literary landmarks. I. Title.
  PS3525.A4152Z85 2015
  813'.54--dc23
  [B]
                        2015030259

Reviewers:
Prof. Dr. Jerneja Petrič (University of Ljubljana)
Prof. Dr. Mladen Knežević (University of Maribor)
Ddr. Natalia Kaloh Vid (University of Maribor)

ISBN 978-3-631-67018-7 (Print)
E-ISBN 978-3-653-06181-9 (E-Book)
DOI 10.3726/ 978-3-653-06181-9

© Peter Lang GmbH
Internationaler Verlag der Wissenschaften
Frankfurt am Main 2016
All rights reserved.
PL Academic Research is an Imprint of Peter Lang GmbH.

Peter Lang – Frankfurt am Main · Bern · Bruxelles · New York ·
Oxford · Warszawa · Wien

All parts of this publication are protected by copyright. Any
utilisation outside the strict limits of the copyright law, without
the permission of the publisher, is forbidden and liable to
prosecution. This applies in particular to reproductions,
translations, microfilming, and storage and processing in
electronic retrieval systems.

This publication has been peer reviewed.

www.peterlang.com

Acknowledgements

Special thanks go to the reviewers of the monograph.
Thank you.

Let's say that in my lifetime, certain things have gotten better and other things have grown worse, so much so that latter-day events would stagger the imagination of the 19th century. If, for example, the flush toilet is an improvement in existence, if the automobile is an improvement, if technological progress is an improvement, then look at the price that was paid. It's not too hard to argue that the gulags, the concentration camps, the atom bomb, came out of technological improvement. For the average person in the average developed country, life, if seen in terms of comfort, is better than it was in the middle of the 19th century, but by the measure of our human development as ethical, spiritual, responsible, and creative human beings, it may be worse. The English language has hardly been improved in the last half century. Young, bright children no longer speak well; the literary artists of 50 and 100 years ago are, on balance, superior to the literary artists of today. The philosophers have virtually disappeared — at least, those philosophers who make a difference.

Norman Mailer, Michael Lennon. *On God: An Uncommon Conversation.* New York: Random House, Paperback edition, 2008, p. 7

Table of Contents

1. Introduction 11
   1.1 Methodology and Literature Review 14

2. The Lives of Norman Mailer 17
   2.1 Biographical Sketch of Norman Mailer 20
       2.1.1 Childhood 20
       2.1.2 Harvard 22
       2.1.3 The Army 23
       2.1.4 The Writer in Need of Inspiration 24

3. Mailer's Works 31
   3.1 A Remarkable Stylist and New Journalist 31
   3.2 America, O, America… 32
   3.3 Fiction Or Non-Fiction? 34
   3.4 Mailer's Ouvre 36
   3.5 Mailer's First Published Novel 38
   3.6 Mailer's Pulitzer Prize Winning Novels – *The Executioner's Song* and *The Armies of the Night* 41
       3.6.1 The Executioner's Song 41
       3.6.2 The Armies of The Night 47
   3.7 Some Other Outstanding Works By Mailer 53
       3.7.1 An American Dream 53
       3.7.2 Miami and The Siege of Chicago 58
       3.7.3 Why Are We in Vietnam? 61
       3.7.4 Of a fire on the Moon 64
       3.7.5 Why Are We at War? 69
   3.8 The Swan Song – The Castle in the Forest 75

4. Mailer's Reception in Europe and Slovenia 77
    4.1   Translations 77
            4.1.1 Mailer in Europe and The Balkans 77
            4.1.2 Mailer in Croatian, Serbian, Macedonian and Slovene ... 78
            4.1.3 Yugoslav Media on Mailer 85
            4.1.4 Mailer is Still of Relevance in The Balkans 90

5. Mailer and Literary Tourism 91
    5.1   Mailer – The Generator of Cultural and Literary Tourism 91
            5.1.1 Literary Tourism 91
    5.2   Legacy Power 93
    5.3   Mailer – His Roots and Travels 95
    5.4   Brooklyn and Provincetown – Mailer's Special Literary Tourism Destinations 99
            5.4.1 Brooklyn 99
            5.4.2 Provincetown 103

Afterword 107

References 109

Pictures 117

Index 119

Reviews of the Monograph 125

1. Introduction

Literary tourism as a type of cultural or heritage tourism is well known today, especially in the United States of America, where Norman Mailer plays a significant role in literary tourism. Today, Provincetown in Massachusetts, for example, is strongly associated to the great American author Norman Mailer. He was one of the greatest men of letters in the second half of the twentieth century, who strongly influenced many areas of American public life (besides literature also journalism and politics), and has become a generator of literary tourism. Yes, recently, literary tourism has been on the rise. Probably because literature in all its varieties and genres is very important not only for literature lovers, literature enthusiasts or professionals and linguists, but for people from all career fields and walks of life. For a number of reasons, literature – and reading for that matter – are vital for everyone. Obviously, reading is an essential skill for functioning in everyday life, for establishing quality relationships, for fulfilling professional responsibilities, and much more. Reading develops the mind, the spirit, and imagination, which in turn hone the creative sides of human personality. This creativity manifests in all areas of life, including economic development.

Literature can be experienced in many different ways. One such mode of experience is literary tourism, which is described in this monograph in connection to the American novelist and journalist Norman Mailer, a great man of letters, who is considered to be one of the most important American authors of the twentieth century, producing some of the best writings of the post-war era. Most of his works depict the complexities of the contemporary American social, political and economic life in a realist mode. Mailer's style, his portraying of the American reality is also illustrated in this monograph using several examples. Mailer portrayed the American Zeitgeist of his time, from the terror of the Second World War, to the dynamic social and political processes of the post-war period, to the moon landing in 1969. Mailer's writing often explores conflicts, particularly the relationship between the individual and the system or the society. In his works, Mailer speaks of the dangers of political power and the power of capital, while calling the attention to the threat of totalitarianism in the United States. During his entire career, he discussed the effects of power, violence, terrorism, sex, the phenomenon of the dictator Adolf Hitler, religion, and corruption, and his works issued continual warnings of the danger of losing freedom and dignity.

This monograph examines the reasons for the importance of Norman Mailer in the world literature and literary tourism by concentrating on the following fictional works: *The Naked and the Dead* (1948), *An American Dream* (1965) and *Why Are We in Vietnam?* (1967). In addition to his fiction, this monograph also considers his non-fiction work, including *The Armies of the Night* (1968), *Miami and the Siege of Chicago* (1968), *Of a Fire on the Moon* (1970), *The Executioner's Song* (1979, by some this novel is considered fiction) and *Why Are We at War?* (2003). The monograph analyzes the areas of contemporary social and political life that were most often critically referred to by Mailer. Freedom, spirituality, nature of human love, critical debate, dangers of conformity etc. are among the most common of his themes. Thus, it can be claimed that Mailer's themes are of general human concern, and consequently, Mailer is one of those authors who promote intercultural and global community.

Mailer could be called 'the critical voice of the United States' for his prolific examination of how good intentions sometimes get lost or compromised in the fight for freedom and democracy. His first novel, *The Naked and the Dead,* was successsful in both the United States and Europe, is a pessimistic account of the Second World War as well as the future of the United States. Mailer observes that the American army and the society are corrupted and crippled by selfishness, inhumanity, violence, brutality, and materialism, calling attention to how devastating these developments are for American society at large. Mailer is critical towards ruling people in power that tolerate, enable, encourage, or reward violence. According to Mailer, American society is threatened by totalitarianism because big corporations are far too influential in the country.

An American Dream renders a critique of the American society. The main topics of Mailer's fourth novel are religion, church, the devil and God, and life after death. The author is convinced that the society in the United States is too dependent on organized religion and the church as an institution, which he believes that is the main reason why people tend to avoid some crucial subjects, like freedom or spirituality. Mailer also criticizes – the church in this novel for representing the wealthy elites and their interests. By comparing Las Vegas to Versailles, linking American to the corrupted world of pre-revolutionary French aristocracy, which allows him to put forth a harsh criticism of American capitalism and consumerism. He raises other crucial questions, among them the issue of abortion and its consequences. In addition to this, Mailer is often very critical of irresponsible reporting and journalism of the mainstream American media.

While Mailer did not believe in the myth of the United States as a promised land, he maintains a firm faith in his homeland. In *The Armies of the Night*, Mailer implies that better future and hope lie in the young generations. As a moral example, he describes the courage of the protesters in the 1967 march against the Pentagon – the American symbol of power. He questions the relationship between history and fiction, once again calling out the kind of reporting presented by American media, who sell fiction as facts. He believes that America is a fundamentally divided society, filled with divisions between the left and the right, the rich and the poor, the young and the old, the whites and the blacks. These divisions weaken – and threaten to destroy – the American society.

Numerous examples of violence committed by the American government are described in *Why Are We in Vietnam?*. In accordance with his self-styled "left-conservatism," the author opposes the war in Vietnam, and believes that the involvement of the United States in Vietnam is not only unjust, and fundamentally wrong, as interfering in foreign affairs and fighting wars in distant countries for dubious reasons was immoral. In *Miami and the Siege of Chicago*, Mailer also reminds the readers that freedom should not be taken for granted; it is something that must be fought for, continuously, day by day. This text deals with numerous other themes and issues, including the youth culture, environmental pollution, and money. This Mailer's book is also an excellent example of how politicians can – and often do – abuse rhetoric. Mailer implies that the politics of the United States has come to display some of the characteristics of totalitarianism.

Despite Mailer's patriotism, his works often reveal a pessimism about the future. The novel *Of a Fire on the Moon* is one such example in which he argues that the driving force of practically everything, including the space technology and space flights, is corporate capitalism. The landing of

Apollo on the moon, according to Mailer, opened the path towards space imperialism, which had an irreversible impact on the future trajectory of the planet because technology now prevails over nature. In Mailer's view, the progress of technology will gradually diminish nature, and thus, jeopardize the future. Self-destruction is often on the author's mind.

Mailer's criticism of divided and complex society of the United States and his political leanings are well seen in *The Executioner's Song*, awarded the Pulitzer Prize, making it both a critical and commercial success. In this novel, the author stresses the lack of basic moral values, along with the violence of the society, the irresponsibility of the mainstream media, and the dilemma of the morality of the death sentence, which for Mailer stands in opposition to the primary value of life.

Why Are We At War? is another book that deals with topics that have accompanied Norman Mailer since his first novel *The Naked and the Dead* in 1948. In this book, the author very clearly articulates his opinion on capitalism, patriotism, totalitarianism, terrorism, and foreign policy of the United States. The fact that a country once used to be a democracy does not at all guarantee that it will be a democracy forever.

After the death of Norman Mailer on 10 November 2007, the legacy of this prominent and world-famous American author continues. Testament to his continuing legacy are the many literary pilgrims who visit his home in Provincetown every year, and his flat in Brooklyn. What is more, Mailer's work continue to reach audiences around the world, whether through critical Mailer studies, or with new translations of his works, which have now been translated into more than twenty languages, among them Chinese, Russian, Slovakian, Slovenian, Bulgarian, Czech, Croatian, Serbian and Macedonian.

As such, this monograph can be used not only as a guide for Mailer's tour in the United Sates in America, but across the world. It is based on interdisciplinary approach, combining scholarly analyses work with interviews with researchers, scholars and translators, and textual analyses of Mailer's works and their translations.

1.1 Methodology and Literature Review

The monograph *Norman Mailer and his Legacy – Literary Tourism: The Case of Norman Mailer* is based on the interdisciplinary approach.

It analyses the role of Norman Mailer in literary tourism in the United States, as well as his reception across the world, with the emphasis on the Balkans. The textual analyses of Mailer's literary works in the first part of the monograph have been combined in the second part with descriptions of places that have come to be associated to Norman Mailer. In this way, the monograph offers a multifaceted perspective on the present-day influence of Norman Mailer both on literary landscape and on literary tourism. This monograph also examines the phenomenon of literary tourism by analyzing existing scholarly research in this area. In addition to this, the methods of interview and data analysis are employed, together with descriptive and inductive methods.

2. The Lives of Norman Mailer

The title of this chapter is not incorrect: Mailer's life was so rich and diverse that his official biographer J. Michael Lennon titled the biography of the American icon *Norman Mailer: A Double Life* (2013). Many biographers attempted to capture Mailer's complex personality, including Richard Poirier in 1972, Philip H. Bufithis in 1978, Hillary Mills in 1984, Peter Manso in 1986 and Mary Dearborn in 2001. By considering all six of the above-mentioned biographies of Norman Mailer alongside his books, articles and other pieces or manuscripts, the most comprehensive picture of Norman Mailer emerges. On the back cover of Lennon's biography of Mailer, Norman Mailer is referred to as "one of the giants of American letters, and one of the most celebrated public figures of his time," but behind this label there are more than 40 fiction and non-fiction books, articles, movies, unpublished materials, more than fifty thousand letters, and more. In addition to this, Mailer was the co-founder of *The Village Voice*, which in its early years "had a greater impact on the non-fiction/journalistic world than any other single publication, with the possible exception of *Esquire* and *The New Yorker*" (Gutking 6), served as the president of the American Chapter of PEN from 1984 to 1985, and was a member of the American Academy of Arts and Letters from 1984 until his death in November 2007.

Among other activities, Mailer was actively engaged in politics. In 1969, he was a candidate in the Democratic primary race for mayor of the New York City, sharing a ticket with the equally outrageous journalist Jimmy Breslin, who was running for president of city council. Their campaign slogan was: "The other guys are the joke!" Mailer received only 41,000 votes (Breslin got 75,000 but still came in fourth of five candidates). Fortunately, Mailer applied his drive and energy with more success in service of the literary community and continued writing.

In his 84 years, Norman Mailer wrote more than 40 books, married six times, fathered nine children, and had ten grandchildren. The dynamic of the Mailer family must have been extraordinary. When some of the members of the Mailer family attended the Eleventh Annual Meeting of the International Norman Mailer Society, Barbara Mailer Wasserman, Norman

Mailer's younger sister, commented on their big family with the following: "…it's amazing to me how well everybody gets along. I think, oddly enough, my own interpretation of … the reason for this is because Norman had so many different wives that there were less sibling rivalry among the children than there might have been if they all had been the product of one father and one mother, for whatever that's worth," and Mailer's children Susan Mailer and John Buffalo Mailer agreed with this observation (B. Mailer et al. 2014: 60–61). They also commented on Norman Mailer stabbing his wife Adele, stating that this event was like a dark shadow that was always somehow there, stretching over Mailer's history (B. Mailer et al. 2014: 66–68).

Norman Mailer experienced many different roles and received many honors for his work, including two Pulitzer Prizes for the *Armies of the Night* and *The Executioner's Song*, respectively. Despite his many awards, however, he never received the Nobel Prize for Literature because according to him "Writing is spooky" (*Spooky* 70) as he titled one of his books in which he reveals his most intimate thoughts on writing and his writing career.

Mary V. Dearborn wrote that "in the case of Norman Mailer, the man and his life are of equal, often competing stature with his work," and that "it is for his life as well as his work that he will be remembered" (Dearborn 8). By using these words she was not exaggerating, and she was not the only one who used superlatives when it came to describing Mailer. Columnist Jimmy Breslin pronounced Mailer as "one of the half-dozen original thinkers in this century" (Dearborn 3). His last novel, *The Castle in the Forest*, was the eleventh of his books to appear on the bestseller list of *New York Times* (nmcenter.org).

Ideologically, Mailer labelled himself "Left–Conservative" (theamericanconservative.com). In his interview for *The American Conservative* in December 2002, he provides an explanation for this apparent oximoron:

> *The idea that a very rich man should not make 4,000 times as much in a year as a poor man. On the other hand, I am not a liberal. The notion that man is a rational creature who arrives at reasonable solutions to knotty problems is much in doubt as far as I'm concerned. Liberalism depends all too much on having an optimistic view of human nature. But the history of the 20th century has not exactly fortified that notion. Moreover, liberalism also depends too much upon reason rather than any appreciation of mystery. If you start to talk about God*

with the average good liberal, he looks at you as if you are more than a little off. In that sense, since I happen to be—I hate to use the word religious, there are so many heavy dull connotations, so many pious self-seeking aspects—but I do believe there is a Creator who is active in human affairs and is endangered. I also believe there is a Devil who is equally active in our existence (and is all too often successful). So, I can hardly be a liberal. God is bad enough for them, but talk about the devil, and the liberal's mind is blown. He is consorting with a fellow who is irrational if not insane. That is the end of real conversation. On the other hand, conservatism has its own deep ditches, its unclimbable walls, its immutable old ideas sealed in concrete. But lately, there are two profoundly different kinds of conservatives emerging, as different in their way as the communists and the socialists were before and after 1917, yes, two types of conservatives in America now. What I call "value conservatives" because they believe in what most people think of as the standard conservative values—family, home, faith, hard work, duty, allegiance—dependable human virtues. And then there are what I call "flag conservatives," of whom obviously the present administration would be the perfect example. I don't think flag conservatives give a real damn about conservative values. They use the words. They certainly use the flag. They love words like "evil." One of Bush's worst faults in rhetoric (to dip into that cornucopia) is to use the word "evil" as if it were a button he can touch to increase his power. When people are sick and have an IV tube put in them to feed a narcotic painkiller on demand, a few keep pressing that button. Bush uses evil as his hot button for the American public. Any man who can employ that word 15 times in five minutes is not a conservative. Not a value conservative. A flag conservative is another matter. They rely on manipulation. What they want is power. They believe in America. That they do. They believe this country is the only hope of the world and they feel that this country is becoming more and more powerful on the one hand, but on the other, is rapidly growing more dissolute. And so the only solution for it is empire, World Empire. Behind the whole thing in Iraq is the desire to have a huge military presence in the near-East as a stepping stone for eventually taking over the world. Once we become a twenty-first century version of the old Roman Empire, then moral reform will come into the picture. The military is obviously more puritanical than the entertainment media. Soldiers can, of course, be wilder than anyone, but the overhead command is a major pressure on soldiers, and it is not permissive. (theamericanconservative.com)

Like his idol Ernest Hemingway, whom he never met in person, Mailer was obsessed with violence and fame. While Hemingway did not stab his wife as Mailer did, Mailer shared Hemingway's machismo and love of women, alcohol, boxing and bullfighting, exhibitionism and controversy. Mailer, in fact, wanted to turn bullfighting and boxing into art, and ultimately succeeded in making machismo, boxing, bullfighting, exhibitionism, and controversy part of his art. In his novel *The Deer Park*, the protagonist

Sergius O'Shaugnessy is a former boxer. In *Advertisements for Myself*, Mailer writes "Isn't the whole point of *boxing* to knock the other guy down and win the bout?" The author mentions boxing and fighting in many of his works, but *The Fight* is famous for celebrating boxing. The novel, which is considered a masterpiece in the literature of sports, is about a boxing fight that took place in Kinshasa, Zaire between Muhammad Ali and George Foreman in 1974. In the book, Mailer presents boxing as a twentieth-century art:

> *It was a study to watch Ali take punches. He would lie on the ropes and paw at his sparring partner like a mother cat goading her kitten to belt away. Then Ali would flip up his glove and let the other's punch bounce from that glove off his head, repeating the move from other angles, as if the second half of the art of getting hit was to learn the trajectories with which punches glanced off your gloves and still hit you; Ali was always studying how to deaden such shots or punish the glove that threw the punch, forever elaborating his inner comprehension of how to trap, damp, modify, mock, curve, cock, warp, distort, deflect, tip, and turn the bombs that come toward him, and do this with a minimum of movement, back against the ropes, languid hands up. (Mailer,* Fight, *5–6)*

Mailer found similarities between himself and some boxers, and he had great admiration for Muhammad Ali. Given this, it is not surprising that Mailer included fighting and boxing in many of his books, including *Tough Guys Don't Dance* and *The Executionr's Song* in addition to the works already mentioned.

2.1 Biographical Sketch of Norman Mailer

2.1.1 Childhood

Norman Kingsley Mailer was born on 31 January 1923, in Long Branch, New Jersey to a Jewish family. His father, Isaac Barnett (Barney) Mailer, emigrated from South Africa, where he had served in the British army. He immigrated to the United States soon after the end of the First World War, where he worked as an accountant and married Fanny (Fan) Schneider, who ran several small businesses. The Mailers lived in middle-class neighbourhoods in Brooklyn, New York. (Bufithis 4, Dearborn 12, Lennon 8–15, Poirier 167).

Fanny adored her son: "I thought Norman was perfect, a really lovely baby. He weighed about seven pounds at birth" (Manso 15). She commented on the provinence of Norman's name, explaining that "Norman was named Nachum Malech. 'Nachum' is 'Norman.' 'Malech' is 'king' in Hebrew. We named him – he was our king. Maybe I was more versed in Hebrew names and words than Barney because of my father, although "Kingsley" is what appears on his birth certificate" (*ibid.*).

Mailer himself joked about his name: "Mailer is an English name, given to my grandparents when they went to South Africa from Russia. Nobody knows what the name was originally. Mailorovski? Mailorovich? Yeah, something out of Dostoevsky! Norman Isaacovich Mailorovsky!" (*ibid.*).

In 1927, when Norman was four years old, the Mailer family moved to Eastern Parkway, a part of Brooklyn, which was, according to the writer, "the most secure Jewish environment in America" (Bufithis 4). In the same year, Mailer got a sister, Barbara (Manso 15).

According to his mother, Norman's talents became apparent very early on in his childhood:

> When Norman started school I would walk him in the mornings, and even in the first grade his teacher recognized his talent and let him write whatever he wanted to. One day she met me outside and I remember her saying, "Mrs. Mailer, you have to realize that your son's pleasures in life are going to be solemn ones.
>
> I was pleased, of course, but it didn't surprise me, because he had already started to read and his nose was always in a book. He didn't start talking earlier than most kids, but he had that quality of making people interested and always had a circle around him, everybody, all the relatives. /.../ He got so much attention from the family that it was like he was a little god. (Manso 16)

Mailer expressed his passion for writing at an early age – penning a story titled *An Invasion from Mars* when he was nine years old. However, aeronautics was his first love. As a child Mailer played the clarinet and saxophone, and spent countless hours making model planes (Bufithis 4–5, Dearborn 14–17). His cousin Marjorie "Osie" Radin described his love to model planes:

> Norman started with model airplanes when he was about ten. He was serious, so serious that his Aunt Anne and Uncle Dave decided he should be an aeronautical engineer, and his parents went along with it. Everybody was very impressed with the building of those airplanes except me. Why? I thought. What good is it?
>
> I remember the models hanging in the living room. Anything that he did had to be on display. Compared to Barbara, Norman was more demanding, but the two

of them were extremely devoted as brother and sister. That kind of relationship had been fostered between my brother and myself, and Fan did the same thing. It was insisted on. There was always great devotion, and we were all close-knit, the entire family. (Manso 18)

2.1.2 Harvard

In 1939, at the age of 16, Mailer entered Harvard University. He majored in engineering, but also pursued his passion for writing by working at the *Harvard Advocate* and studying under English faculty members Robert Gorham Davis, Robert Hillyer, and Theodore Morrison. Mailer's short story "The Greatest Thing in the World" won the 1941 *Story* magazine college contest and brought him to the attention of several editors and publishers. (Bufithis 5, nmcenter.org). At the time, also Mailer's appearance was outstanding:

> */.../ Mailer was also physically underdeveloped, a short, scrawny youth, only five feet seven, with ears that stuck out awkwardly from a small, narrow triangular face. The halo of curls that would become so familiar in later life was clipped in short, wiry waves. "He had none of the manner of the grand seigneur that he has now," says Bowden Broadwater, a fellow member of the Harvard class of '43. (Mills 38)*

Despite the fact that in 1939, one-fifth of all freshmen at Harvard were Jews, Mailer and his fellow Jewish students felt excluded from the student body:

> *Most public-school Jews at Harvard, Mailer included, were painfully aware that freshman year of being outside the existing social order. The subtle distinctions of dress, manner, lineage, and wealth that made up a Harvard "gentleman" eluded them, while the boys from Groton, St. Paul's, or Milton, who considered Harvard a continuation of their privileged prep school days, instinctively knew how the system worked and which activities to join. /.../ At Harvard in 1939 it was standard practice not only to isolate incoming Jewish freshmen by assigning them rooms together but to group the prep-school graduates as well, making it difficult for newcomers like Mailer to absorb the intricacies of the Harvard establishment, especially the club and house systems.* (Mills 40–41)

His time at Harvard had a major impact on the future writer. He began to read works by Wolf, Faulkner, Fitzgerald and Hemingway, and firmly decided to become a major American novelist. As a student, he wrote a short story "The Lady Wears a Smile" and in the summer of 1941, the novel *No Percentage*, which was not published. Mills describes this work in relation to Mailer's early life and relationship to his mother:

> *No Percentage* was probably an outgrowth of Mailer's relationship with his strong-willed mother, Fanny Schneider Mailer. Throughout his life Fanny influenced her son more profoundly than any other person, and she has remained the only one to whom Mailer willingly defers. Although at Harvard Mailer was actively engaged in growing beyond his nice-Jewish-boy-from-Brooklyn image, and even though his novel pilloried suffocating parents, he would never break his ties with Fanny. (Mills 54–55)

His first short story "The Greatest Thing in the World" was published in *The Harvard Advocate*. The influences of Farrell, Dos Passos and Steinbeck can be seen in this early work (Bufithis 5–6, Mills 44).

After the Japanese attack on Pearl Harbour in December 1941, the United States entered the war on the side of the Allies. Young Mailer accepted the inevitability of war and decided to seize on the unfolding events as impetus to write the first American novel about the Second World War. One of Mailer's friends, Seymour Breslow, commented on Mailer's decision 'to go to war' as both a solider and a writer: "Rather than thinking about the horror of war or the fact that he might get killed, he looked at it as an experience which would feed the novel he wanted to write afterward. He was desperately searching for experience at the time, because he came to the realization that you can't write if you don't experience" (Mills 60).

Mailer graduated from Harvard in June 1943. After completing his degree, he wrote another unpublished novel titled *A Transit to Narcissus* based on his observations of a psychiatric hospital in Boston (Poirier 167, Bufithis 6).

2.1.3 The Army

In March of 1944, he married his college girlfriend, Beatrice Silverman (the couple had a daughter Susan, born in 1949), and was drafted into the Army, where he was assigned to the 112th Cavalry Regiment in the Philippines and assigned to perform various duties, including reconnaissance patrols. After the Japanese surrender, Mailer served as a cook in occupied Japan until his discharge in May 1946. (Bufithis 6–7, Mills 66–67, nmcenter.org). It seems that to Mailer the War was a useful experience. He did not shy away from hard work, nor did he use his Ivy-League education to gain advantage in the military. As Beatrice recalls: "As Harvard graduate Norman could have become an officer, but he preferred to go in as a private because he felt that if he was made an officer, he would be put behind a desk and never see combat" (Mills 75–76). But to be able to write about the war, he wished to experience it. Because he served as an infantryman, he was faced with greater danger. On fearing for life during the war, Mailer said: "At a certain point you get awfully tired as an infantryman – not because you're in combat all the time, but just because it's a tough life: it's like being a dishwasher. Your horizons come down and down and down, until you don't much care whether you remain alive or not. So I really did give up the idea that I'd ever come back and be a writer" (Mills 79).

Mailer's army experience was the basis for his 1948 novel *The Naked and the Dead*, which he wrote while living in the suburbs of Provincetown. Nominated for the Pulitzer Prize and The Gutenberg Award, the book brought Mailer literary fame and great financial success (Mills 80–81).

The ideas for the big novel were born during the war. Mailer wrote them down while he was serving, and sent them in letters to his first wife Beatrice, who described her husband as a workaholic, not the kind of person who would wait for inspiration and planned his work meticulously: "Norman was a very obsessive type of writer, not inspired. Everything was worked through: how many chapters, what would happen in each chapter" (Mills 82).

2.1.4 The Writer in Need of Inspiration

After *The Naked and the Dead* was published, journalist Orville Prescot from *New York Times* wrote: "/.../ the most impressive novel about the second World War that I have ever read. /.../ Mr. Mailer is as certain to become famous as any fledgling novelist can be" (Mills 100). For 11 weeks, the novel was the best-selling book in the United States. (Mills 102–106). Mailer believed that his literary success was a matter of circumstance—and luck:

> Large literary success is so often a matter of fortuitous publication. The Naked and the Dead had the luckiest timing of my career. By 1946, people were no longer that interested in novels about the Second World War. But The Naked and the Dead didn't come out until 1948, and by then readers were ready. If it had appeared earlier, I don't know that it would have had equal impact. (Mailer, Spooky 55)

When he looked back on the publication two years after the release of *The Naked and the Dead*, he went on to say:

> *I never thought of it being an antiwar book, at the beginning. But every time I turned on the radio and looked in the newspapers, there was this growing hysteria, this talk of going to war again, and it made me start looking for the trend of what was happening. It seemed to me that you could get men to fight again. They came out of the war frustrated, filled with bitterness and anger and with no place to focus their anger. They would begin thinking, "I don't give a goddamn. I'll go into it, at least it'll be a change!"* (Mills 84–85)

By the early 1950s Mailer had separated from Beatrice. He cited his growing success as the main reason for their divorce:

> *She was a very strong woman. She profoundly resented the female role into which my success had thrust her. You see, when we married, she was, if anything, stronger than me. She was perfectly prepared to go out and work for years in order to make enough money for me to stay at home and write a good many books. And if that happened, we probably would have been a happy couple of that sort, she the strong one, I the gentle one. Then what happened? I became successful so suddenly I got much more macho. /.../ I suddenly felt like a strong man. That altered everything between us.* (Mills 124)

His second novel *Barbary Shore* (1951) received bad reviews. And although his third novel, *The Deer Park* (1955), was reviewed more favourably, Mailer increasingly branched out into other forms of writing, particularly journalistic pieces and essays. In the early 1950s he began writing for magazines such as *Dissent, Esquire,* and *Partisan Review,* and in 1955, he helped co-found *The Village Voice,* a free weekly news and culture magazine in New York. In these and other periodicals, Mailer commented on race, feminism, sexuality, politics, literature, art, culture, and society. In 1959, he published a collection of these essays, with additional fiction and commentary, titled *Advertisements for Myself,* which he explained as the form where he really found his voice as a writer: "I thought that was, oddly enough, the first book written in what became my style. I never felt as if I had a style until that book. When I developed that style, for better or for worse, a lot of other forms opened to it" (Mills 194).

In 1954, Mailer married Adele Morales (they had two daughters together: Danielle and Elizabeth), and moved to Mexico. In 1960, at a party, Mailer stabbed her, not by accident as witnesses told later:

> *One evening at a party at the Mailers, there was a sense of impending violence. During the evening Adele and Tina Bourjaily went into the kitchen to prepare food. As Adele was slicing salami with a large knife, she began talking to Tina and gesticulating with her hands. Mailer suddenly came into the kitchen through a swinging door, and by sheer accident Adele's knife was pointing directly at his stomach. Mailer looked at his wife and said, "You don't dare, baby." Norman was playing, but they were always playing their little games. (Mills 151)*

Despite sustained a severe injury, Adele did not wish to press charges. Mailer received court probation and public condemnation, and his second marriage ended (Mills 217–218).

In the early 1960s, Mailer was trying to stabilize his life and strengthen his literary reputation. In 1962, he was briefly married to Lady Jeanne Campbell, a daughter of Ian Douglas Campbell, 11th Duke of Argyll. Mailer and Lady Jeanne had a daughter Kate together. According to Mills (270), Mailer said: "I was crazy about her – she's a great girl. But the choice came down to this: Either she became a good wife and took care of my four children, or I became Mr. Lady Jeanne. Our two worlds were pretty far apart. /.../ Lady Jeanne gave up ten million dollars to marry me, but she would never make me breakfast." This marriage was followed by another marriage, to the actress Beverly Bentley, with whom he had two sons Michael and Stephen. During this tumultuous period in his personal life, he published a volume of poetry, *Deaths for the Ladies (and Other Disasters)* in 1962, and his fourth novel, *An American Dream* in 1965. It seems that this period was extremely important to Mailer, and that it shaped his style considerably. And this was also the period, when a new literary technique, a new literary style, called New Journalism, emerged. This new literary genre combined literary and journalism writing techniques, and emphasized the importance of the truth. Also Hilary Mills argues that Mailer's discovery of his own style and voice coincides with the beginnings of New Journalism. Mailer himself commented on his contributions to New Journalism with the following words:

> *These days everyone is laying claim to having started the New Journalism. Truman Capote is screaming. Tom Wolfe has been writing manifestos about it for the last ten years. And Lillian Ross, who actually started it, has been silent. But I think that if I started any aspect of that New Journalism – and I did – it was that of an enormously personized journalism in which the character of the narrator was one of the elements in the way the reader would finally assess the experience. I had felt*

> *that I had some dim intuitive feeling that what was wrong with all journalism is that the reporter tended to be objective and that that was one of the great lies of all the time.* (Mills 194–195)

1960s were successful also in relation to awards. Mailer received the Pulitzer Prize and the National Book Award for his novel *The Armies of the Night* (1968).

In the late 1960s, Mailer made three experimental films: *Wild 90*, *Beyond the Law*, and *Maidstone*. Later, in 1982, he wrote the television adaptation of *The Executioner's Song* and later on wrote and directed a major studio production of his 1984 novel *Tough Guys Don't Dance*. He performed minor roles in several films and television programs and wrote the television screenplays for *American Tragedy* and *Master Spy: The Robert Hanssen Story*.

In 1980, after his divorce from Beverly Bentley and a very short marriage to jazz singer Carol Stevens, who is the mother of his daughter Maggie, Mailer married the painter Norris Church (formerly Barbara Davis). They remained married until his death. Norris and Norman had a son together – John Buffalo, and Mailer informally adopted Norris's son Matthew Norris from her previous marriage. According to biographers and even Mailer's mistresses, Mailer had a number of extra-marital affairs during his marriage to Church. The most famous of his mistresses is Carole Mallory, a model and an actress, who also wrote a book *Loving Mailer* about her affair with the famous author, which lasted almost eight years. In her book, Mallory admitted: "When Norman ended our relationship in 1991 I felt as though a limb had been amputated. Gradually, over the following ten years, time would heal my cavernous wound." (2009: 195) In *A Double Life*, Lennon (595) states that in addition to Mallory, Mailer was also having affairs with Carol Stevens, Eileen Fredrickson, Lois Wilson and others. Norris Church suffered greatly because of these affairs, as she always found out about them sooner or later (Lennon: 594). She referred to herself as Mailer's "last wife," the title she gave to herself when people asked her which wife she was. Mailer's infidelities, however, were not the only problem in their marriage: there were ex-wives and his children, alimony and school tuition to be paid, all of which added up to substantial financial pressures. Adulteries were not Mailer's only sins. According to Witchel (2010), Mailer made plenty of mistakes outside of his many failed and fraught marriages as well: he became friends to a convicted murderer Jack Henry Abbott, who was imprisoned again less than two months after his release, again on murder charges, he drunk too much, and he brought his old girlfriends home for dinner.

As far as Mailer's relationships to women are concerned, he strongly opposed abortion and was also against contraception (Smith, theguardian.com). He frequently displayed degrading and violent behavior towards the women in his life, including stabbing his wife Adele and beating his fourth wife Beverly Bentley. His writing, in turn, often demonstrates inappropriate behavior and attitudes towards women is portrayed in common themes ranging from violence, domestic abuse, abortions, and degrading sex.

Mailer spent his last years in Provincetown, Massachusetts – writing. In 2007, he published his last novel *The Castle in the Forest,* and a few weeks before his death in New York his work *On God: An Uncommon Conversation,* the book he co-authored with Michael Lennon. Mailer died on 10 November 2007 because of acute renal failure in Mount Sinai Hospital in Manhattan.

In 2010, Norris Church, who died on 21 November 2010 in New York, published a book of memories from her life with Norman called *A Ticket to the Circus.* She also had previously published two novels, *Windchill Summer* (2000) and *Cheap Diamonds* (2007). On Mailer's last summer when he was still actively writing but also suffering from health problems, she wrote:

> Every evening at six, after an afternoon of writing in our studios, Norman and I would meet in the bar next to the living room for a glass of wine. We'd look out at the sea and the boats in Provincetown Harbor, watch the gulls, and talk. After a lifetime of booze – bourbon and gin and rum, scotch and vodka – now Norman liked red wine mixed with orange juice, a mild sangria punch, while I sipped a dry Kir on ice – soda pop wines, a taste of sweet, a drop of alcohol, to help us unwind. Those were hard, slow days, the last days of summer 2007. Norman was still writing, but fighting to breathe, and I had my problems, too. Eternity was on our minds a lot of the time when we talked. "I wonder if people will remember me when I'm gone," Norman would frequently muse. "Will they continue to read my books, do you think? Or will they just forget me?" (N. C. Mailer 3)

Norris Church Mailer also commented on the fact that Mailer never penned his autobiography:

> I think for years he might have intended to do it, but there was always another book that took his fancy, and, finally, he was surprised to realize that he had run

> *out of time and that he really hadn't wanted to do it at all. As he said more than once, he was sick of himself and didn't want to analyze himself anymore – he had done too much of it. Even narcissists have limits, it seems.* (N. C. Mailer 423)

Since there is no published autobiography by Mailer, we have more biographies about him and more opportunities for speculation about his life (lives). It is probably not an exaggeration to speculate that the last biography of Norman Mailer has not yet been written. He was a writer, a journalist, a critic, a soldier, an actor, a producer, a politician, an outlaw, a father and a husband. He experienced many roles, and thus it can justifiably be stated that Mailer, indeed, had such a rich life as if he had lived several lifetimes.

3. Mailer's Works

3.1 A Remarkable Stylist and New Journalist

Norman Mailer was a literary journalist (literary journalism is a type of literature that combines reporting based on facts with the narrative techniques, characteristic of literature), more precisely, a new journalist (reporting about real-life events in complex-styled stories, this type of literary journalism emerged in 1960s), and what is most important, Mailer was a remarkable stylist, and according to Collins "the quintessential American chronicler and critic" (2014: 94). To some extent, his style was influenced by his predecessors and literary idols, including John Steinbeck, James Farrell and John Dos Passos. Some readers and critics received Mailer's style positively, while others criticized his occupation with form. As Joan Didion wrote: "It is a largely unremarked fact about Mailer that he is a great and obsessed stylist, a writer to whom the shape of the sentence is the story" (Lennon 79). Dickstein states that "Mailer had a genius for description, for evoking atmosphere" (2007: 123), and Yalkut points out that "Mailer's journalism has been justifiably lauded for its perspicacity, breadth of vision, and daring use of novelistic techniques" (2013: 204). Regarding the debates concerning the so-called "New Journalism" of the 1960s and 1970s, which wrestled with questions about distinction between fiction and nonfiction, objectivity and subjectivity, Yalkut argues that Mailer's achievement in the context of American journalism history has been overlooked, asserting that "Mailer's most significant, lasting and influential work may in fact be his journalism, particularly his early journalism."

> What first strikes a journalism historian in Mailer's nonfiction is the virtuosic uses to which he puts the oral tradition – fittingly enough, since the oral, exclamatory style goes back to the very origins of news: one person telling another what happened. Everyday American speech has been part of American literature and journalism since the days of the early Republic and the frontier, of course. The Southwestern humourists relied on dialect for their rollicking effects, as did that gifted lecturer Mark Twain, who actually read his work out loud as he was writing and made sure that his readers listened: in the prefatory note to Huckleberry Finn, for example, Twain enumerates the six dialects he has "painstakingly" used in the novel. /.../ Norman Mailer has managed to go beyond the compassionate

> *Twain and the enraged Mencken: Mailer makes obscene language literary.* (Yalkut, 2013: 204–205)

Mailer contributed significantly to the development, establishment and popularization of literary journalism, both within the United States and abroad. According to the characteristics and the fashion of the literary movement Mailer subtitled his novel *The Armies of the Night* (which is an example of 'participatory journalism', i. e. when the author is part of the events described) with *History as a Novel, the Novel as History*, he additionally explained the title of the book *Miami and the Siege of Chicago* with *An informal history of the American political conventions of 1968*, and he himself called *The Executioner's Song true life story*. Many scholars who have dealt with the theory of literary journalism, such as Wolfe, Mosser, and Lennon have recognized Mailer for his unique contributions to this field.

3.2 America, O, America …

The United States of America is at the center of Mailer's work, and his writing often attempts to understand his home nation, and his relationship to it. Power and conflict are his main themes, ranging from his personal conflicts with the United States to the conflicts fought between the United States and foreign countries. Thus, it can be said that Mailer's works reflect the Zeitgeist of the United States during the second half of the twentieth century. As critic Morris Dickstein says:

> Mailer's dialogue with his age can be gauged not simply in relation to public events like the Vietnam War, the 1967 protest march on the Pentagon, the moon shot, or the feminist movement. Mailer tangled with each of these in turn, as he had engaged with the second world war, the cold war, the Hollywood blacklist, and the Kennedy campaign. What was more important was how his work, as keenly attuned to the Zeitgeist as to his own obsessions, reflected the inner turmoil of his times. (Dickstein 123)

Mailer's works comprise a sort of a documentary perspective into American society. Gabriel Miller supports this claim:

> It seems clear that the Norman Mailer of the past twenty years is more comfortable in the realm of non-fiction, where the demands of social and political reality force him to keep a tighter rein on the extravagant energies of his imagination. In works such as The Armies of the Night (1968), Of a Fire on the Moon (1971), and The Executioner's Song (1979), Mailer's narrative talents and his prodigious

capacities as an observer of American social and political life merge into a fluent and compelling whole. (Miller 80)

Among the authors of the American post-war generation, Mailer is certainly the one who wrote the most prolifically about the United States of America, and was also the most critical towards his home country. In his works, he presents a complex picture of American society, uncovering and questioning the attitudes of the Americans towards contemporary events and some controversial decisions made by those in power. His works serve as a kind of mirror that reflects society back at its readers, prompting them to reconsider their role in big issues of the day.

In addition to the political and social critique rendered by Mailer, Mosser (2014: 109) also comments on the function of his language, pointing out that his "use of slang had political purposes and consequences," and adds that Mailer's writings display "fresh coinages" (Mosser 2014:108). One of the most interesting 'Mailerisms,' according to Mosser (*ibid.*), is the word "fug", which he uses frequently instead of "fuck" in his first novel *The Naked and the Dead*.

According to Begiebing, who calls Mailer "provocateur-in-chief", the "great theme in much of Mailer's fiction and nonfiction is courage – the discovery and retention of one's courage (or the failure to do so)" (2013: 404). Mailer's works insist that Americans need to become more aware of the pressing issues facing the nation because that is the only way they can improve themselves and their country. According to Mailer, the only way America will become a better country, a real democracy, is without rushing into the abyss, deceived by its own glorified picture of the global superpower, who has the right to regulate the world in their own image. Regarding Mailer's descriptions of America, Wenke wrote: "Throughout his career he has written with an acute sense of the millennial assumptions that helped create from the very beginning of the country a uniquely American consciousness" (237). According to Wenke's analysis, Mailer discovered "more about America than any of his contemporaries, having had the moral courage and artistic integrity to write about the threat of totalitarianism in the land of the free and the home of the brave" (238). Mailer believed that his mission was to write about the outer realities, the realities and issues of the real world. Busa also argues that the famous author "always maintained that the first duty of a novelist was not to write about himself, but about another self that he feels comfortable inhabiting" (2014: 317).

Wenke's recognition of Mailer's political and artistic activism further strengthens the argument about Mailer's prominent standing in American literature presented in this chapter. For these reasons, Wenke considers Mailer one of the most important American authors: "The sustained quality and range of his work place him well within the first rank of American prose writers that includes Faulkner, Melville, James, Hawthorne, Emerson, Hemingway, Fitzgerald, Twain, Poe, and Thoreau" (*ibid.*).

3.3 Fiction Or Non-Fiction?

With Mailer, the question of whether his work qualifies as fiction and non-fiction often arises. In literature, however, the boundary between reality and fiction is difficult to determine: despite whether a certain work is considered non-fiction or documentary, that is, written on the basis of facts, the literary creation is still ultimately a subjective one. This leads to the question as to whether the works of literary journalism belong to the artistic or non-artistic literary journalistic discourse. Foley locates the documentary novel on the border between the discourse of facts and fiction discourse, but does not believe that the boundaries between these two discourses should be erased (1986: 25). As Foley describes, "The documentary novel approaches the frontier between fictional and non-fictional discourse, but it does not transgress or blur that borderline. /.../ The documentary novel's insistence that it has a particular truth to tell thus reinforces rather than undermines fiction's distinct status as a means of telling the truth" (Foley 267–268).

There is also the dilemma as to whether Mailer's works should be classified as literary journalism, as New Journalism, as high or low culture, or to put it differently, as art in opposition to popular culture. According to Wolfe, the exceptional power of New Journalism stems mainly from the four techniques: (1) an exact description of the scene of events; (2) exact replica of dialogues of the protagonists; (3) third-person position (presentation of each scene through the eyes of a certain character, so that the readers get the feeling that they are inside the character's head and that they are experiencing the events the same as the character); (4) imitation of everyday habits, gestures, behaviour, customs, description of housing equipment, clothing, decorations, mode of travel, nutrition, maintenance of houses, and a description of other details that are relevant to show the status of the characters' lives (1996: 46).

In literary discourse, the aesthetic function can be dominant, but it need not be the only function, as literature exists for more than simply to satisfy our sense of the beautiful. For instance, a literary text may exist only because the author had the need to express themselves, as opposed to journalistic texts, which must always inform or interpret. Journalistic texts have an additional function. At linguistic and stylistic levels, literature and journalism can meet, even join. Texts that combine features of literature and journalism are usually referred to as literary journalism, or New Journalism. Therefore, a simple definition of literary journalism would be that it combines the best of both literature and journalism: literary writing style along with journalistic credibility and a commitment to conveying the truth. When deciding to combine literature and reality, literary journalists tend to use the argument that the real life is more interesting and fascinating than fiction, and that readers want to read about reality. It could be argued that literary journalism is about people's lives, not only about the events that make the headlines. Literary journalism therefore goes beyond strict reporting of the news according to the rules and conventions of standard journalism. Connery, who divides literary journalism into different periods, believes that the news aspect of literary journalism is based on writing at a given time, with real people and scenes, but the literary aspect of the work will endow it with enduring value that will also make it interesting and meaningful for readers in the future (1992: 15).

It should be noted, however, that the reader plays a key role in deciding whether a work is fiction or non-fiction. Mosser also points out the central importance of the reader by citing W. R. Winterowd:

> *Literariness, fictionality, and poeticality are not functions of the text itself but result from the way in which the reader takes the text, using the appropriateness conditions that constitute the genre. If the reader takes the nonfiction novel to be nonfiction, the essential conditions for assertions would apply: the work would be taken as representing an actual state of affairs. Under this condition, the obviously fictional elements in a text—such as invented dialogue—are taken as authorial interpretations, legitimate hypotheses about reality, not as fictions [....]. (42)*

It can be argued, therefore, that in spite of the characteristics of literary journalism and New Journalism, the text is not the one which a priori possesses the characteristics of New Journalism. Instead, the reader's perception of the text and way of reading are also determining factors.

3.4 Mailer's Ouvre

Mailer's ouvre is comprised of hundreds of manuscripts, screenplays, more than 50,000 letters and more than 40 books of fiction and non-fiction, including:

The Naked and the Dead (1948)
Barbary Shore (1951)
The Deer Park (1955)
The White Negro (1957)
Advertisements for Myself (1959)
Death for the Ladies (And Other Disasters) (1962)
The Presidential Papers (1963)
An American Dream (1965)
Cannibals and Christians (1966)
Why are we in Vietnam? (1967)
The Armies of the Night (1968)
Miami and the Siege of Chicago (1968)
Of a Fire on the Moon (1970)
The Prisoner of Sex (1971)
Maidstone (1971)
Existential Errands (1972)
St. George and the Godfather (1972)
Marilyn (1973)
The Faith of Grafitti (1974)
The Fight (1975)
Some Honourable Men (1976)
Genius and Lust (1976)
The Transit of Narcissus (1978)
The Executioner's Song (1979)
Of Women and their Elegance (1980)
Of a Small and Modest Malignancy (1980)

Pieces and Pontifications (1982)
Ancient Evenings (1983)
Tough Guys don't Dance (1983)
Harlot's Ghost (1991)
Portrait of Picasso As a Young Man (1996)
Oswald's Tale (1996)
The Gospel According to the Son (1997)
The Time of Our Time (1998)
Why Are We At War? (2003)
Modest Gifts: Poems and Drawings (2003)
The Spooky Art: Thoughts on Writing (2003)
Norman Mailer's Letters on An American Dream, 1963–1969 (2004)
The Big Empty, co-authorship with John Buffalo Mailer (2006)
The Castle in the Forest (2007)
On God: An Uncommon Conversation, interview collection, co-authorship with Michael Lennon (2007).

MOTION PICTURES: *Wild 90,* 1968, Crime Drama; *Beyond the Law,* 1968, Drama; *Maidstone: A mystery,* 1971, Drama; *Tough Guys Don't Dance,* 1987, Murder Mystery; *The Executioner's Song,* 1982, Mini-series TV drama; *American Tragedy,* 2000, Mini-series TV drama; *Master Spy,* 2002, mini-series TV drama (http: //www.mailerlicensing.com/).

Rhodes reports that in 2007, Cinemalta, which is a French company, released Mailer's early films on DVDs: *Wild 90, Beyond the Law,* and *Maidstone* with subtitles (2013: 435), the latter being "Mailer's most fully realized and important film" (Rhodes, 436).

All the publications and artistic achievements listed above belong to one artist. Or as Collins put it:

> *There you have him: critic · prophet · journalist · essayist · novelist · psychologist · rebel · trickster · and street philosopher all packaged tightly together in the body of a Jersey-born · Brooklyn-raised · curly-haired · blue-eyed · impulse-driven · risk-prone · short-tempered · fast-speaking · quick-witted · Harvard-educated · Army-trained · Freudian-influenced · sex-driven · Monroe-fixated · boxing-obsessed · anti-establishment · anti-technology · anti-war · anti-feminist · little barrel-chested of a man with a colossal swagger that exposed his arrogance and insecurity. (2014: 95)*

Readers, critics and scholars have listed and arranged Mailer's works according to various criteria and made different rankings of Mailer's best books. J. Michael Lennon, Mailer's official biographer and friend, distilled Norman Mailer's career, rich in genres, into his best books in the following order, starting with best regarded: *The Executioner's Song*; *The Armies of the Night*; *An American Dream*; *Advertisements for Myself*; *Harlot's Ghost*; *The Naked and the Dead*; *The Fight*; *Why Are We in Vietnam?*; *Marilyn*; and *The Time of Our Time*. This monograph, however, will concentrate on Mailer as a social critic in different periods of his writing career, and thus on the following books: Mailer's first published book, *The Naked and the Dead*, the two Pulitzer Prize winning novels *The Executioner's Song* and *The Armies of the Night*, as well as *An American Dream*, *Miami and the Siege of Chicago*, *Why Are We in Vietnam?*, *Of A Fire on the Moon*, and *Why Are We At War?*. A note on Mailer's last novel *The Castle in the Forest* is also included because this novel rounds the author's career.

3.5 Mailer's First Published Novel

This monograph presents an analysis of Mailer's socially critical works and begins with Mailer's debut novel *The Naked and the Dead*, which became an immediate hit after its publication in 1948 and logged record-breaking sales. It also received critical acclaim, with critics declaring the young author a significant new American writer. According to Mills, Prescott described *The Naked and the Dead* in *The New York Times* as "the most impressive novel about the Second World War that I have ever read. /.../ Mr. Mailer is as certain to become famous as any fledgling novelist can be" (100). Although not all critics recognized Mailer's first novel as a major work, one point they did agreed upon was that the author showed promising. David Dempsey's review on May 9, 1948 in *the New York Times* stated: "*The Naked and the Dead* is not a great book, but indisputably it bears witness to a new and significant talent among American novelists" (nytimes.com). Even though it is a debut work, *The Naked and the Dead* has proven to be an extraordinary novel with the passage of time, as it still resonates strongly with readers today. More than two decades after its initial release in 1974, the critic Alfred Kazin wrote: "Probably still the best novel about Americans at war, 1941–1945" (Glenday 197). It should be mentioned that before the publication of this novel, Mailer did have a considerable amount of experience as a writer, and by 1948 had already written many articles, stories, and even unpublished books (including *No Percentage* and *A Transit to Narcissus*).

The Naked and the Dead is set in the Second World War. Written in the style of naturalism with elements of symbolism, it describes the struggles between the American soldiers and the Japanese on one of the Philippine Islands, which the author called Anopopei:

> *In the early briefing of his staff, Major General Edward Cummings, commander of the troops on the island, had described Anopopei by saying it was shaped like an ocarina. It was a reasonably accurate image. The body of the island, about a hundred and fifty miles long and a third as wide, was formed generally in a streamline with a high spine of mountains along its axis. On a line almost perpendicular to the main body of Anopopei, the mouthpiece, a peninsula, jutted out for twenty miles. (Mailer, Naked 36)*

Perhaps it would be an exaggeration to claim that the fictional island of Anopopei, which is described in detail in the above citation, is a microcosmic representation of the United States. However, the U.S. military could be interpreted as the metaphor for the fragmented American society, which had found itself in a crisis from which there is no easy exit.

American soldiers are still fighting wars in foreign territories, far from home, and the military system has not changed significantly. It seems that Mailer was right in warning that American society is built on false values, since it was these values that led the country to new crises. Seven decades after the release of Mailer's first novel, the events of the Second World War described in the debut probably lost some of their immediate resonance with readers due to the passage of time, but the message of the book remains strong because the writer's pessimistic predictions indeed come true, as Mailer himself probably had not even imagined as literature often uses exaggeration to picture some facts more obviously. Mailer's message says that during the war, only the external enemy was beaten. The internal enemy, something much more dangerous, remained undefeated, and resulted in corruption, selfishness, stupidity, greed and cruelty. Thus, the spirit of the novel is pessimistic.

As this is often the case with Mailer, this work is not interesting solely because of the topics it covers. It also feature an incredibly polished style.

Glenday explains that some critics pointed out "the political and philosophical correspondences between the novel and its antecedents in the leftist American literary scene of the 1930s" (199). Glenday also adds: "In its stress upon deterministic views of human behaviour, and its realisation of a world in which the individual is dehumanised and subjected to the efficient functioning of entrenched systems of control, *The Naked and the Dead* may seem a somewhat stale recapitulation of a vision and a style inappropriate to a changed postwar world" (*ibid.*). Glenday further warns that "one should not be misled by the novel's dated style since Mailer's concern is not primarily retrospective, /.../ but is rather prophetic" (199) and he compares Mailer to Saul Bellow, whose first novel *Dangling Man* was published in 1944. According to Glenday (199–200), Mailer and Bellow both conclude their books ironically, "the war fought for freedom and democracy has somehow contrived to undermine the appeal of these ideals" (*ibid.*)

Glenday's observations on Mailer's debut novel are somehow prophetic, and require additional attention. *The Naked and the Dead* is a remarkable novel about the Second World War, and repeated readings confirm that while the narrative may be set in the past, it is simultaneously a gloomy prediction of the future. Given that this is a novel about war, it cannot be overlooked that Mailer devoted very little attention to the actual Japanese, whom the Americans were battling in the Pacific. Instead, he was more interested in the internal enemy, that is, everything that paralyzed the army from within. Mailer draws attention to the inhumanity, dehumanisation, excessive materialism, and pathology of power, which is embodied in military structures, along with inequality and violence in human relations. The novel can be read as a tale offering a great view of American society, an intriguing insight into the great America; the military system and the army serve as a metaphor for the modern social structure, even a new social order. Mailer is concerned with power and its relationship to violence. With the precise depiction of the battalion, the author offers insight into the army, by displaying an inhumane totalitarian machine, which in turn symbolically represents totalitarianism in American society, which is considered as one of the most democratic societies in the world.

The directness so typical of Mailer's entire career is also very present in his first novel, *The Naked and the Dead*. The nudity aluded to in the title refers to the process of dehumanization, the horrors of war, the vulnerability of soldiers, and powerlessness. Desires and aspirations are completely subordinate to the military system, and the military structure is shown as an inhumane, totalitarian apparatus. Individuals do not reach their goals, or they achieve them only partially, and there are thus major losers in this system. Morris Dickstein commented that "Mailer had felt the shadow of some form of postwar fascism" (2007: 120).

By depicting American soldiers as his protagonists and relating their life stories, Mailer effectively paints a fragmented and ethnically mixed American society. Much like this multicultural American society, the U.S. military is also highly fragmented, consisting of different groups of people – from descendants of Irish and Polish immigrants to immigrants from Mexico.

In *The Naked and the Dead*, the author clearly shows that the American soldiers belong to minorities who differ from the majority population. To Mailer, this is a clear sign that American society has not yet attained the highly coveted American dream in a land where there are supposed to be equal opportunities for all.

Norman Mailer's debut novel contains issues and topics that would follow the author through his entire career: human pathology (violence, power, Hitler phenomenon, twisted and rough sexuality), the Jewish question, terrorism, religion, inequality and corruption.

Mailer's first novel is actually a drama about human inhumanity and (in)human character. Despite a handful of good people, the world is doomed, according to Mailer's first novel. While the plot line of *The Naked and the Dead* depicts war, his critical exploration of the military system and the machinery of war result in a profoundly anti-war message.

3.6 Mailer's Pulitzer Prize Winning Novels – *The Executioner's Song* and *The Armies of the Night*

3.6.1 The Executioner's Song

The Executioner's Song was published in 1979. It is a novel that according to Lucas "speaks loudly with Mailer's voice" (2013: 418) and is still considered one of Mailer's best books (at least according to Mailer's biographer J. Michael Lennon, and the author of this monograph). It won the Pulitzer Prize in 1980 not only for its great literary value; it also presented a new literary approach to non-fiction. The novel is comprised of two long parts – of two books, actually: Book One or "Western Voices," and Book Two or "Eastern Voices." The "Eastern Voices" section is comprised of the voices of influential people, mostly men, and the voices in "Western Voices" are mostly women, as Joan Didion pointed out in her 1979 review of *The Executioner's Song*. Each book further on consists of seven parts, which are further subdivided into chapters, with Book One consisting of 32 chapters and Book Two of 44 chapters. While over 100 different characters appear in the novel, the protagonist is Gary Mark Gilmore, a thirty-five year old male who had been paroled from the United States Penitentiary in Marion, Utah, who tries to resume a normal life, but he just does not succeed. Since he suffers from severe headaches, he takes drugs all the time. Gary comes from a dysfunctional family, and is the second of four sons, the first three of whom suffer sad fates: the first son is murdered, Gary is sentenced to death and shot, the third ends up in the asylum, and the fourth becomes a writer.

The book explores Gilmore's backstory leading to his eventual execution. Due to events in his childhood, he was emotionally underdeveloped. He left school at fourteen, and a year later he led a gang of car thieves. Several times he was put in correctional homes or prisons for minors, where he had much time to read, study, write songs. During short periods of freedom, he was an angry and impatient young man who wanted to satisfy his needs and desires immediately. If he could not get what he wanted, he would simply steal or rob to get it. After Gilmore was released from prison in Marion, where he served because he committed a robbery, on April 9, 1976, he found a job, established some social contacts, and entered into a relationship with the nineteen-year old Nicole Baker. Soon, Gilmore continued with minor criminal acts, and one day, after quarrelling with his girlfriend Nicole, something changed and his violence turned deadly serious. On July 19, 1976, he murdered a man named Max Jensen at a gas station in Orem. The next day his deadly rage poured out on a motel manager named Ben Bushnell in Provo. He was arrested the same day. The trial, which occurred several months later lasted only two days, but the court sentenced him to death. Gilmore stated he did not know why he murdered those people. In prison, he wanted to die as soon as possible and did not want his death sentence to be commuted to a life sentence. This surprised the authorities and the public, because in the United States at that time, according to Mailer, public opinion was not in favour of executions. Gilmore stood firm with his request. Twice he tried to commit suicide, both times unsuccessfully. He was finally executed in Utah by firing squad on January 17, 1977 in the first execution in the United States in ten years. According to Vince, "this death has become the symbol of something more lasting, raising significant legal, cultural, and religious issues – issues that continue to haunt the United States" (2014: 293).

The first part of the novel describes Gilmore's childhood and his numerous experiences with the correctional institutions and later on, prisons. Gilmore's parole from prison before the murder is described in detail. The second book reports extensively of Gilmore's trial, about his objections to being spared the death penalty, the lawyers' efforts to save Gilmore from the death penalty despite his opposition, and on the copyright business with Lawrence Schiller, who is one of the main characters in part one of the novel. As Mailer stated in the last part of the novel, Schiller carried out the majority of interviews with Nicole Baker. In terms of the structure of the novel, Vince argues that "all the traditional literary elements – character, story, plot, theme, metaphor – weave in and out, dancing together – rather as particle and wave do in contemporary physics" (2014: 295).

In 1980, Mailer won the Pulitzer Prize for fiction for *The Executioner's Song*, the second in his career as a writer. This honor put his work in the public spotlight, and debates on the novel's genre were popular for some time. In 1982, a film adaptation of the book was produced, directed by Lawrence Schiller. Gary Gilmore was played by Tommy Lee Jones. In the so called 'non-fiction novel,' which he wrote over the period of a year and a half, Mailer gathered personal stories of more than a hundred people, which allowed him to create a documentary portrait of Gilmore's life. The reader gets a detailed, disturbing, and intimate perspective into the murderer's life and fate.

Given its hybrid genre, *The Executioner's Song* was promoted both as "a novel" and as "a model of precise and accurate reporting" (Fishkin 208). In the afterword of the novel, Mailer claims that *The Executioner's Song* is "a factual account" and "as accurate as one can make it" (1053) given its foundation in interviews conducted with over 100 people, relevant documents, records of court rulings and other original materials. It is estimated that research on which the novel was based span approximately

1,500 pages. (Mailer, *Song*, 1051). In the afterword, Mailer also expresses thanks to the many individuals who contributed to the work, especially to Nicole Baker, who is a key figure of the novel. Mailer believed that without her help, the novel would have been impossible to write. She was willing to share details about her intimate relationship with Gilmore with Schiller, who interviewed her first, and then with the writer, which proved to be very valuable for the novel. Most interviews with Nicole Baker, as described in the last part of the novel, were performed by Lawrence Schiller. According to Lennon, "Mailer wanted it both ways: accrue every benefit of factuality and historicity –"this really happened" – while adding fictional immediacy and interiority" (2013: 530).

The Executioner's Song was a new milestone in Mailer's career. It was published at a time when some critics and readers had written the writer off, as Bufithis argues, because he was writing "in the same way" (2007: 77). "When *The Executioner's Song* appeared in 1979, they reconsidered" (*ibid.*). What is more, Bufithis compares Mailer's novel to *Crime and Punishment* by Fyodor Mikhailovich Dostoevsky (78), one of the masterpieces of Russian and world literature.

Disregarding the comparisons, it is an indisputable fact that crime and punishment stand at the core of this novel, certainly in a different time and space than Dostoevsky, but with *The Executioner's Song*, twentieth-century America got its own *Crime and Punishment*.

The author himself commented on both the real and fictional elements in *The Executioner's Song*. He believes that acquired secondary materials, such as quotations from newspapers, permitted some artistic freedom. At several points, he omitted words or phrases without any indication, for example also in the letters. Several times he modified the word order in sentences or replaced the order of the paragraphs. The writer made decisions to modify facts to achieve better readability and enhance the plot, he also admits that some facts were changed, or are fictional (Mailer, *Song*, 1052). Readers who are aware that the novel is a non-fiction literary work may ask themselves while reading the novel: what is true, what is not, what is added to the facts? Such questioning can be interesting and invigorating while reading. To Mailer, style was an important issue also in this novel.

Mark Edmundson (2003) compares the style of *The Executioner's Song* to that of Waldo Ralph Emerson:

> One way to think of The Executioner's Song is as a book in which Mailer, willingly or under some compulsion, enters the prison of a restricted style. He surrenders the freedom of Emersonian abandonment and encloses himself in the rectangular walls of the book's isolated paragraphs. He adopts a voice that is cold, flat, and spectral and makes the acquiescence to death his central principle of value. The style is terminal. (Edmundson 137)

Media reports, especially articles from various newspapers represented valuable materials for both Mailer and Lawrence Schiller, who helped a great deal with collecting the novel materials. The author incorporated media news and follow-up stories on Gary Gilmore into the novel, especially in Book Two, thus providing more objective and credible information to the reader. Mailer also gives the reader insight into the world of American media at the end of the 1970s, shedding light on the logic behind the kind of thinking of those working in the media, as well as the possibility of creating public opinion and influencing it. According to the novel, media in the United States was very strong at the end of the 1970s and because of the reporting in the media, which launched partial information, some corporations and individuals made huge profits. Even in the media capitalist thinking was present, which was evident from the pragmatic behaviour of editors and journalists. They were all under pressure and were willing to do almost anything to do a story on Gilmore, for his letters, interviews with Nicole Baker, and with his family members and acquaintances, including stalking, waiting in front of the house, tracking people, etcetera. The characteristics of the media industry are well outlined in the last third of the novel, during which the negotiations between Lawrence Schiller and Gary Gilmore for exclusive copyright of his life story are depicted.

The Executioner's Song is also a story about a divided America. The formal structure of the book, which is divided into "Eastern" and "Western Voices," reflects the content examined in the novel relating to American socioeconomic stratification and the gaps between social classes.

Truman Capote (Grobel 2000) held that Mailer's novel is fiction because Mailer did not investigate the story by himself, and he wrote about people and things second hand, as originally reported by others, particularly Schiller. Lennon states that "over three hundred people have speaking parts in *The Executioner's Song*, and Schiller had dealings with 99 percent of them"

(2013: 534). Lennon further on comments on Mailer's decision to include Schiller in the book:

> But his decision to extend the ambit of his narrative and present a full portrait of Schiller was dictated not only by Schiller's centrality, but also by Mailer's desire to give the reader something that Capote purposely omits: the story of the story. (Lennon, 534)

However, Mailer's novel has different dimensions than Capote's. One important difference is that Mailer never met the main protagonist of his novel Gilmore, unlike Capote, who conducted extensive interviews with the two criminals profiled in *In Cold Blood*. When discussing the fictional elements of *The Executioner's Song*, the question of the 'second-hand' truth arises. Is this still the truth or is it modified and interpreted to such an extent that it can no longer be called the truth? Much of the information in Mailer's novel came through intermediaries. The key question is whether those parts of the novel in which Mailer describes the thoughts and feelings of the convicted person are indeed more fiction than fact. Even if the reader believes that Schiller and Mailer are empathetic towards Gilmore, it is impossible to truly know the innermost thoughts and feelings of a convicted person who wants to be executed as soon as possible. For these reasons, the novel is fiction – far from an objective documentary.

For today's reader, *The Executioner's Song* remains of interest because it explores eternal philosophical questions about the meaning of human life, love, death, life after death, good and evil, violence, relationships, money, politics, punishment, death penalty, ethics etcetera. What is the value of human life? Is Gary Gilmore also a good and compassionate man, despite being a murderer? Why is the literary protagonist a murderer, and not his victims? etc. The characters of the novel try to provide some answers to these questions, emphasizing that there is good and evil in every person.

Furthermore, this novel is also valuable to contemporary readers because it forces readers to think and evaluate. Today, the United States is in many ways different from the country in 1979, when the novel was published. However, the scenes of violence, such or similar as described in *The Executioner's Song*, have not disappeared in America.

One of the central questions of *The Executioner's Song* deals with the death penalty. Gilmore's trial in the United States sparked heated debate both in favour of and against the death penalty. Mailer clearly expressed his view that every human life is precious, and he was clearly against the death penalty, characteristic of his left conservatism. On the other hand, on online forums appear opinions that with *The Executioner's Song* and a detailed description of the cold-blooded murders of Gary Gilmore in the novel, Mailer provided the best possible defense of the institution of the death penalty.

In the spirit of his left conservatism, Mailer also renders harsh criticism of the complex and fragmented American society, a place with questionable values. *The Executioner's Song* is a masterpiece. Or as Vince puts it, "a well-crafted Mailer sentence" (2014: 303) – an extremely long one, for that matter.

3.6.2 The Armies of The Night

The Armies of the Night (1968) depicts the anti-war demonstrations that took place in Washington from October 21–23, 1967. Mailer actively participated in these demonstrations as a speaker and was even arrested. His descriptions of events are accurate, detailed and in some parts fascinating. It is interesting that the writer himself, as the main protagonist, still chooses to narrate in the third person, making the novel a good example of participatory journalism. An interesting number would also occur if we counted the number of times the word 'Mailer', which the author repeats as often as possible, appears in this Mailer novel. Some descriptions are very detailed and vivid, drawing the reader into the demonstration:

> *The trumpet sounded again. It was calling the troops. "Come here," it called from the steps of Lincoln Memorial over the two furlongs of the long reflecting pool, out to the swell of the hill at the base of Washington Monument, "come here, come here, come here. The rally is on!" And from the north and the east, from the direction of the White House and the Smithsonian and the Capitol, from Union Station and the Department of Justice the troops were coming in, the volunteers were answering the call. They came walking up in all sizes, a citizen's army not ranked yet by height, an army of both sexes in numbers almost equal, and of all ages, although most were young. Some were well-dressed, some were poor, many were conventional in appearance, as often were not. The hippies were there in great number, perambulating down the hill, many dressed like the legions of Sgt. Pepper's Band, some were gotten up like Arab shieks, or in Park Avenue's doormen's greatcoats, others like Rogers and Clark of the West, Wyatt Earp, Kit Carson, Daniel Boone in buckskin, some had grown mustaches to look like Have Gun, Will Travel – Paladin's surrogate was here! – and wild Indians with feathers,*

a hippie gotten up like Batman, another like Claude Rains in The Invisible Man – his face wrapped in a turban of bandages and he wore a black satin top hat. A host of these troops wore capes, beat-up khaki capes, slept on, used as blankets, towels, improvised duffel bags; or fine capes, orange linings, or luminous rose linings, the edges ragged, near a tatter, the threads ready to feather, but a musketeer's hat on their head. One hippie may have been dressed like Charles Chaplin; Buster Keaton and W. C. Fields could have come to the ball; there were Martians and Moon-men and a knight unhorsed who stalked about in the weight of real armor. There were to be seen a hundred soldiers in Confederate gray, and maybe there were two or three hundred hippies in officer's coats of Union dark-blue. They had picked up their costumes where they could, in surplus stores, and Blow-your-mind shops, Digger free emporiums, and psychedelic caches of Hindu junk. There were soldiers in Foreign Legion uniforms, and tropical bush jackets, San Quentin and Chino, California stripped shirt and pants, British copies of Eisenhower jackets, hippies dressed like Turkish shepherds and Roman senators, gurus, and samurai in dirty smocks. They were close to being assembled from all the intersections between history and the comic books, between legend and television, the Biblical archetypes and the movies. The sight of these troops, this army with a thousand costumes, fulfilled to the hilt our General's oldest idea of war which is that every man should dress as he pleases if he is going into battle, for that is his right, and variety never hurts the zest of the hardiest workers in every battalion (here today by thousands inplaid hunting jackets, corduroys or dungarees, ready for assault!) if the sight of such masquerade lost its usual happy connotation of masked ladies and starving children outside the ball, it was not only because of the shabbiness of the costumes (up close half of them must have been used by hippies for everyday wear) but also because the aesthetic at last was in the politics – the dress ball was going into battle. Still, there were nightmares beneath the gaiety of these middle-class runaways, these Crusaders, going out to attack the hard core of technology land with less training than armies were once offered by a medieval assembly ground. The nightmare was in the echo of those trips which had fractured their sense of past and present. If nature was a veil whose tissue had been ripped by static, screams of jet motors, the highway grid of the suburbs, smog, defoliation, pollution of streams, overfertilization of earth, anti-fertilization of women, and the radiation of two decades of near blind atom busting, then perhaps the history of the past was another tissue, spiritual, no doubt, without physical embodiment, unless its embodiment was in the cuneiform hieroglyphics of the chromosome (so much like primitive writing!) but that tissue of past history, whether traceable in the flesh, or merely palpable in the collective underworld of the dream, was nonetheless being bombed by the use of LSD as outrageously as the atoll of Eniwetok, Hiroshima, Nagasaki, and the scorched foliage of Vietnam. The history of the past was being exploded right into the present: perhaps there were now lacunae in the firmament of the past, holes where once had been the psychic reality of an era which was gone. Mailer was haunted by the nightmare that the evils of the present not only exploited the present, but consumed the past, and gave

> *every promise of demolishing whole territories of the future. The same villains who, promiscuously, wantonly, heedlessly, had gorged on LSD and consumed God knows what essential marrows of history, wearing indeed the history of all eras on their back as trophies of this gluttony, were now going forth (conscience-struck?) to make war on those other villains, corporation-land villains, who were destroying the promise of the present in their self-righteousness and greed and secret lust (often unknown to themselves) for some sexo-technological variety of neo-fascism. (Mailer, Armies 108–110)*

In his novel *The Armies of the Night*, Mailer does not paint a bleak picture of the fate of his country. On the contrary, he still believes that there is hope for the future for the United States because there are still people with strong values. Mailer gives the example of moral courage of the protesters, the so-called "Armed Forces" in front of the Pentagon. According to Mailer, hope for the future rests mainly in the hands of young people:

> *At any rate, we have an army of at least 35.000 amateur soldiers consisting of doctors, dentists, faculty, veterans groups, housewives, accountants, trade unionists, Communists, Socialists, pacifists, Trotskyists, anarchists, artists, and entertainers, no, even historians may have a joke – there was no more than a smattering and a sprinkling of such professionals at the Pentagon. Present in the majority were college students from all over the East, and high school students and hippies and Diggers and bikers. (Mailer, Armies 274)*

Mailer's criticism is often reinforced by his patriotism. Wenke also supports this statement, saying that "the deep well of patriotism from which his bitter criticism of America has always sprung" (1987: 150). Due to the fact that the author disagrees with the involvement and complicity of the United States in these wars, Mailer is faithful to his principles and maintains that criticism is always welcome and necessary because it ultimately leads to progress.

In 1968, the *New York Times* critic Kazin wrote: "I believe that it is a work of personal and political reportage that brings to the inner and developing crisis of the United States at this moment admirable sensibilities, candid intelligence, the most moving concern for America itself. Mailer's intuition in this book is that the times demand a new form. He has found it" (nytimes.com).

Kazin further on points out Mailer's patriotism:

> *The book cracks open the hard nut of American authority at the center, the uncertainty of our power – and, above all, the bad conscience that now afflicts so many*

> Americans. Armies of the Night is a peculiarly appropriate and timely contribution to this moment of the national dramas, and among other things, it shows Mailer relieved of his vexing dualities, able to bring all his interests, concerns and actually quite traditional loyalties to equal focus. The form of this diary-essay-tract-sermon grew out of the many simultaneous happenings in Washington that weekend, out of the self-confidence which for writers is style, out of his fascination with power in American and his fear of it, out of his American self-dramatizing and his honest fear for his country. (nytimes.com)

Kazin called *The Armies of the Night* a 'diary-essay-tract-sermon.' The book represents a genre shift in Mailer's career as he replaced the "traditional" novel with the so-called non-fiction novel, which blurs the line between fiction and journalism. With this new novel, Mailer clearly entered the realm of literary journalism, New Journalism and participatory journalism, which he actively contributed to in the coming decades. For additional style diversification Mailer employed third person narrative technique to discuss himself:

> On a day somewhat early in September, the year of the first March on the Pentagon, 1967, the phone rang one morning and Norman Mailer, operating on his own principle of war games and random play, picked it up. That was not characteristic of Mailer. Like most people whose nerves are sufficiently sensitive to keep them well-covered with flesh, he detested the telephone. Taken in excess, it drove some psychic equivalent of static into the privacies of the brain; so he kept himself amply defended. He had an answer service, a secretary, and occasional members of his family to pick up the receiver for him – he discouraged his own participation on the phone – sometimes he would not even speak to old friends. Touched by faint intimations of remorse, he would call them back later. He had the idea – it was undeniably oversimple – that if you spent too much time on the phone in the evening, you destroyed some kind of creativity for the dawn. (Mailer, Armies 14–15)

Using the third person voice is intriguing. In *The Spooky Art* Mailer discussed the influence of Henry Adams on his writing, especially on employing this third person voice:

> The influence of Henry Adams on The Armies of the Night is peculiar. I had never read much Adams. In my Freshman year at Harvard, we were assigned one long chapter of The Education of Henry Adams, and I remember thinking at the time what an odd thing to write about yourself in the third person. Who is this fellow, Henry Adams, talking about himself as Henry Adams? I remember being annoyed in that mildly irritable way Freshmen have of passing over extraordinary works of literature. To my conscious recollection, I hardly ever thought about him again. Yet, start reading The Armies of the Night, and immediately you say – even

> I said – "My God, this is pure Henry Adams." It's as if I were the great-grandson. Contemplate, therefore, how peculiar is influence: Adams must have remained in my mind as a possibility, the way a painter might look at a particular Picasso or Cezanne and say to himself, "That's the way to do it." Yet the influence might not pop forth for twenty or thirty years. When it does, the painter could say, "Oh yes, that was a Picasso I saw at MoMA twenty-five years ago, and I've always wanted to try such a palette, and now I have." In effect, that's what happened with Henry Adams. (Mailer, Spooky 99)

The novel is comprised of two books: Book One: The Steps of the Pentagon is subtitled "History as a Novel," and Book Two: The Battle of the Pentagon is subtitled "The Novel as History." Each book has 11 chapters, however, Book Two is longer. Book One is "a personal history which while written as a novel was to the best of the author's memory scrupulous to facts, and therefore a document" (284). Book Two is similar to news coverage or journalist reportage, or according to Mailer, "condensation of a collective novel" (284), in which the information from different sources is collected, and then converted into the story.

The author also attempts to show the relationship between fiction and history, alluding to the fact that history and fiction do not differ as much as one might imagine. History is written by winners, and is therefore not necessarily fair or true. By comparing history to fiction, Mailer also draws attention to the problem of the mass media, which often sell fiction as fact to the audiences. Mailer was critical towards the growing and increasingly dominant role of the mass media, which is commented upon in the following excerpt from of Book Two: "The mass media which surrounded the March on the Pentagon created a forest of inaccuracy which would blind the efforts of an historian; our novel has provided us with the possibility, no, even the instrument to view our facts and conceivably study them in that field of light a labor of lens-grinding has produced" (Mailer, *Armies* 245–246).

Bloom also points to the relationship between the novel and history, stating that "once one comes to recognize the true story as a replica of or metaphor for truth, then history becomes a more reliable record, capable of being distinguished from ideological practice" (191). According to Dickstein, the book is "both a great self-portrait and a remarkable snapshot of the historical moment, one taken at a curiously tilted angle. It is at once a book about nothing (in the *Seinfeld* sense) – digressive, meandering, self-indulgent – and the best portrait of the times" (Dickstein 128).

Mailer depicts America as a split society. His so-called left-conservatism is also embodied in the novel, and can be seen in Mailer's perspective on drugs, hippies (25), and the liberal academic parties he despised (29) despite attending them. There is not only the conflict concerning the war in Vietnam, but a series of bitter recognitions that America is anything but the American dream. The society of the United States is divided: left and right, rich and poor, young and old, black and white. The march in front of the Pentagon also reveals all of these contradictions; Mailer even calls the protesters the "Crusaders" (109). According to Mailer, the true symbol of American strength is Pentagon, not the Congress, which is only a tool to achieve the Pentagon's objectives:

> *In Rubin's opinion, Congress was not a source but a servant of the real power in America. So Congress did not inspire the thought of real confrontations between real enemies, it did not stir the imagination to awe and dread and admiration. In fact, for good or ill, Congress was an agreeable symbol to the vast majority of Americans. Rubin had therefore brought another idea. On the West Coast they were talking of a March on the Pentagon which would encircle it, invest it, disrupt it, and conceivably paralyze its actions for a few days. Such a move would have symbolic meaning in America and around the world, for the Pentagon was the symbol of the American military, and so was hated wherever U.S. forces were resented or despised at home or abroad. (Mailer, Armies 252)*

Mailer's novel demonstrates the pathology of power in the United States and illustrates the power of large corporations that operate in the background and have a disproportionate impact on American's lives:

> *Now recapitulate the problem at the Pentagon: an enormous office building in the shape of a fortress housed the military center of the most powerful nation on earth, yet there was no need for guards – the proliferation of the building itself was its own defense: assassination of any high official in the edifice could serve only to augment the power of the Pentagon; vulnerable to sabotage, that also could work only for the fortification of its interest. High church of the corporation, the Pentagon spoke exclusively of mass man and his civilization; every aspect of the building was anonymous, monotonous, massive, interchangeable. (Mailer, Armies 255)*

The author's America is not only a land of great contrasts, but also a country of humour and obscene language, the stylistic particularities to which

Mailer stays faithful throughout his literary career, from his debut novel *The Naked and the Dead* to his last novel, *The Castle in the Forest*.

Additionally, in *The Armies of the Night*, Mailer is not a mere critic, but a patriot, since his constructive criticism primarily stems from his patriotism. According to Dickstein, the novel deals mainly on patriotism, protest and resistance, topics which "feel surprisingly contemporary" (Dickstein 130). Yalkut also comments on how Mailer presents himself in the novel, and states that *The Armies of the Night* "is one long apologia for Mailer's mistakes, faults, and failures /.../" and that "Mailer is constantly explaining the good reasons for his numerous mistakes, enumerating how often he makes a fool of himself, if not an outright buffoon" (2013: 214). On the other hand, what is extraordinary in the novel is its style. Jason Moser calls attention to Mailer's special style – the variety of different voices of a writer who is always present:

> Mailer speaks in numerous voices of his own: there is Mailer the reporter, reporting facts, conveying information; Mailer the social critic, attacking complacency on the left and totalitarianism on the right; and Mailer the prophet, dimly foretelling, as we shall see in the conclusion, the future of America. (Mosser 131)

Mosser's observation is correct, because heteroglossia (inclusion of different discourses in a particular work) is characteristic of Mailer, not only in *The Armies of the Night*, but also in many other of his works, including *The Executioner's Song*.

3.7 Some Other Outstanding Works By Mailer

3.7.1 An American Dream

An American Dream (1965) is Mailer's fourth novel, which he wrote monthly for the magazine *Esquire*, and was then published by Dial Press. The protagonist of the novel is Stephen Richards Rojack from New York, an author and a war hero who after World War II went into politics, and was a violent bully. Leeds highlights the fact that Rojack was also an amateur boxer, who murders his wife, is sleeping with her maid, fights jazz musicians, but still remains unpunished (2002: 65).

Considering the fact that the novel was written several years after the writer stabbed his wife Adele, during the period after separating from Lady Jeanne Campbell, this book can also be read as a kind of confrontation between Mailer and his alter ego. According to Mills (271) and Manso (374), the character of Cherry was also based on Mailer's fourth wife, the actress Beverly Bentley. *An American Dream* is a fantasy novel of sorts, – centering on a perversion of the American dream and the pursuit of sex, violence, crime, the wealth, power and glory. Gordon wrote that "the plot is deliberately riddled with bizarre coincidences and irrational and magical events – all the logic of a dream" (1980: 14).

While Joan Didion labelled *An American Dream* as a "big book" (83) and Barry H. Leeds called it a "masterpiece of character study" (74), the novel was criticized by some critics. Dickstein, for instance, states that the novel was seen as "dime-store Dostoevsky, a megalomaniacal account of 'crime without punishment,' and, moreover, a tasteless, misogynistic play on Mailer's own brush with murder and madness a few years earlier" (2007: 122). Elizabeth Hardwick even labelled it "a very dirty book – dirty and extremely ugly" (Wenke 98). Such reduction of the novel, which describes a subconscious thirty-two hour trip, and explores the hero's inner and outer reality, is not justified. The novel is first and foremost a social critique. Of course, it is a multi-faceted critique, allowing for a number of interpretations – and also the possibility of misinterpretation. A similar comment is made by Kaufmann, who says: "*An American Dream*, with its tantalizing cluster of images, metaphors and near-symbols, is a novel of suggestion, not explanation, a trap for any critic or reader on a symbol hunt" (2007: 201).

In *An American Dream*, "much is implied" and "little [is] substantiated" (Kaufmann 201). The external reality could be understood as a represesentative of the United States, a country, far from the dream, bad in its essence, and so bad, in fact, that Rojack wanted to free himself from it – symbolically – by murdering his wife. It is true that Mailer's choice to leave Rojack unpunished is problematic. In the novel Rojack was questioned by the police several times, but there were not enough evidence to prove him guilty. At this point, it again becomes possible to draw parallels with Mailer's life, who also was known for violent rages, such as the instance when he stabbed his wife Adele. Like his character, Mailer too escaped punishment.

Kaufmann, for example, recognized the literary value of *An American Dream*. According to him, the novel represents a turn in Mailer's career:

> Mailer's An American Dream does not focus on the gross Dream of an America crisscrossed with telephone wires and television antennas, whose fad of the sixties is the conquest of the moon. Rather Mailer's novel, based on total cultural delicacies, is a dramatic critique on those nuances underlining the ambigous values in contemporary America, on those individual roots of American aspirations and ideals. (194–195)

His marriage to Deborah, which Mailer called "a devil's contract" (1965/1969: 24) correlates with Rojack's decision to lead an immoral life in an affluent society without high values, such as honesty, loyalty and fairness. Using this bad marriage as a correlary for weak and problematic social, economic, political and military structures, Mailer is able to make a criticism of U.S. society:

> Our marriage had been a war, a good eighteenth-century war, fought by many rules, most of them broken if the prize to be gained was bright enough, but we had developed the cheerful respect of one enemy general for another. So I had been able to admire the strategic splendor of leaving me in our apartment. It stifled her, she explained to me, it was a source of much misery (Mailer, American 26)

Marriage to Deborah, which for Rojack was like living in a 'corrupt' society, robbed the protagonist of his manhood and dignity. His wife even humiliated him for his war experience: "'God, you're a whimperer,' said Deborah. 'Sometimes I lie here and wonder how you ever became a hero. You're such a bloody whimperer. I suppose the Germans were whimpering even worse than you. It must have been quite a sight. You whimpering and they whimpering, and you going pop pop pop with your little gun' (1965/1969: 28). With these words, she crossed the threshold of her husband's tolerance and effectively signed her death sentence. The murder of his wife was depicted as liberating to Rojack.

According to Joseph Wenke, murdering his wife was Rojack's only chance to achieve redemption: "Despite a long history of /.../ cruelty and hatred, Rojack cannot simply leave Deborah, for he is trapped by a polarity of destructive emotions. Living with Deborah, Rojack is murderous; trying to separate from her, he is suicidal. He can extricate himself from this trap only by fully engaging in the war with Deborah and winning it" (Wenke 97). Although, according to Mailer, Rojack is aware of the possibility that he might be haunted by his deed and that perhaps, *in the hour of his death*, he will meet Deborah again:

> *I did not feel a thing. Which is not to say that nothing was happening to me. Like ghosts, emotions were passing invisibly through the aisles of my body. I knew I would mourn her on some distant day, and I would fear her. I had a certainty this instant that Deborah had been divided by death – by whatever fraction, what was good in her had been willed to me (how else account for the fine breath of this calm) and every last part which detested me was collected now in the face she showed for her death – if something endured beyond her dying, something not in me, it was vengeance. That delicate anxiety which pulses up to flutter in the nose was on me now. For Deborah would be there to meet me in the hour of my death. (Mailer, American 43)*

In the book, murder is condemned as a major crime, but it is also an action necessary for Rojack to save himself, his soul. Murder can be understood as salvation, the symbolic end of an era. Wenke also believes that with murdering Deborah, "he severs his most significant relationship with the society that has seduced his soul". What is more: "He renounces all of the compromising roles that for so many years have been counterfeiting his identity, and he gives himself a chance to find out what the real identity is." (Wenke 97). According to Leeds, "Rojack's murder of Deborah, whether viewed literally or allegorically, cuts him loose from the girdling structures of external identity that have held him up, and sets him on the path of the outlaw" (55). Rojack made a rotten compromise in the novel, and he made personal committments to continue his life differently:

> *Though killing Deborah represents Rojack's greatest renunciation of compromise, it likewise establishes a moral obligation for him to make the renunciation complete, requiring him to do battle with society on every level of his relationship with it and emerge victorious. Such a confrontation would force society to drop its mask and reveal itself as the demon that it really is, a demon personified by the man Rojack fears most: Barney Kelly. (Wenke 98)*

Leeds argues that Rojack's progress is

> *a peculiarly American one, a repudiation of the false American dream of meretricious corruption and an embracing of a new, true American dream of authenticity of self. Rojack comes to represent what was best in the American character after World War II, what was shamelessly corrupted, and what Mailer suggests may be redeemed by courage, discipline and a commitment to selfless heterosexual love. And he does this with the aid of representatives of marginalized groups: Shago and Cherry. (2002: 66–67)*

In this novel, Mailer deals with the role of religion in society, the church, God and satan, and with the afterlife. The novel has a distinctly Manichean (dual) character, since God and the devil struggle for good and evil in the human soul from the beginning to the end of the novel: "Since the Church refuses to admit the possible victory of Satan, man believes that God is all-powerful. So man also assumes God is prepared to forgive every last little betrayal. Which may not be the case. God might be having a very bad war with troops defecting everywhere. Who knows? Hell by now might be no worse than Las Vegas or Versailles" (*American* 221).

This novel can be read as a critique of society that relies too much on faith and the Church, which diverts people's attention from important issues. Even though Mailer himself was a Jew, he was very critical towards Judaism: "I always say it takes one Jew to do in another" (235). By comparing Las Vegas with Versailles, the novel aligns the American Sin City with the depraved, corrupt world pre-Revotionary France, a world primarily concerned with the accumulation of wealth. It is this historical comparison that allows Mailer to further his critique of the American form of capitalism and consumerism. Among other things, he mentions Karl Marx: "Remember you once said Marx said, 'Quantity changes quality'?" (133).[1]

In the novel Mailer also writes on issues of sex and adultery, abortion and responsibility for the unborn child. It should be noted that this topic came to the forefront of public discussions during the civil rights and feminist movements that gained traction during the 1960s and 1970s. In *An American Dream*, he writes:

> "*You ever pregnant before?*" "*Yes.*" "*Kelly?*" "*Yes.*" "*What happened to the child?*" "*I didn't have it.*" "*Any other time?*" *She was silent.* "*Shago Martin?*" "*Yes.*" "*Afraid to have it?*" "*Shago was afraid to have it.*" "*How long ago?*" "*Three months.*" *She nodded.* "*Three months ago. And last week I broke up with him.*" /.../ "*And you didn't want to have it by yourself?*" "*I didn't have the guts. You see, I had cheated on him.*" "*With Tony?*" "*Yes.*" "*Why?*" "*Habit, I guess.*" (Mailer, American 166–167)

Here, Mailer implicitly indicates that American society is not merely totalitarian, but also incestous. It turns out that the father of Rojack's stepdaughter Deirdre, who is illegitimate daughter of Deborah, Barney

---

1 Mailer often used the idea that the amount impacts the quality, for example in *Of a Fire on the Moon*: "(As Marx/Engels had been the first to point out: quantity changes quality)" (182).

Kelly, is Deborah's father: "'Yes, I killed her,' I said, 'but I didn't seduce her when she was fifteen, and never leave her alone, and never end the affair,'" (Mailer, *American* 236). In this novel, Mailer utilizes both conventional and unconventional forms of sexuality. And according to Leeds, "In *An American Dream*, Rojack is linked to his demonic adversary, Barney Oswald Kelly, by the fact that each has had sexual relations with Deborah, Ruta, and Cherry" (2002: 78).

"In *An American Dream*, Mailer took a cliché (as indicated by his title) and made of it an allegorical indictment of American society" (Leeds 2002: 84). Because the novel is permeated by tragic atmosphere, the title echoes and plays on the title of the 1925 novel *An American Tragedy* by Theodore Dreiser. At the end of the novel, the main protagonist Rojack departs the country, with plans to find new hope in Guatemala, and Yucatan.

3.7.2 Miami and The Siege of Chicago

In *Miami and the Siege of Chicago*, Mailer describes the differences between the Republicans and the Democrats, which are also reflected in the choice of the city in which the parties prepared their conventions: the Republicans in Miami and the Democrats in Chicago. In this novel, the author is a reporter, unlike in *The Armies of the Night*, where he writes about himself in the third person and is the main protagonist (insider): "The reporter took out his notebook and stood in front of one of these Jeeps and took notes of the dimensions. /.../ The reporter had, after all, studied engineering at Harvard." (Mailer, *Miami* 210).

Although Mailer is predominantly a 'reporter', he also refers to himself with his real surname several times throughout the novel, mostly to reference his literary achievements and unique style:

> *The reporter met Bobby Kennedy just once. It was on an afternoon in May in New York just after his victory in the Indiana primary and it had not been a famous meeting, even if it began well. Senator came in from a conference (for the reporter was being granted an audience) and said quickly with a grin, "Mr Mailer, you're a mean man with a word." He had answered, "On the contrary, Senator, I like to think of myself as a gracious writer." (Mailer, Miami 194–195)*

For the contemporary reader, the book has lost some of its timeliness because Mailer describes and analyzes the political situation in the United

States in 1968. Still, *Miami and the Siege of Chicago* remains a valuable document detailing the political arena at the end of the 1960s, which reveals a lot about America (like current politics, American internal and foreign affairs). He also explains some basic rules of politics:

> Politics is property; property relations are law-abiding. Even seizure of property can be accomplished legally. So the history of a convention must concern itself with law-abiding citizens; conversely, a study of law-defying citizens who protested the deliberations of this convention in the street ought to find them propertyless, therefore not in politics. In fact, it does not. Not quite. (Mailer, Miami 128)

Mailer outlines a whole range of President Nixon's rhetorical approaches, which are displayed as simple and remote from reality: "The first civil right of every American is to be free from domestic violence" (77); "Our goal is justice for every American" (ibid.); and "America is a great nation today" (ibid.). Nixon promised opportunities for all children to obtain the best possible education, regardless of their origin, family background, or residence in rural areas. Nixon even abused the "I have a dream" rhetoric of Martin Luther King (78). The point here is that in the presidential campaign of the United States, rhetoric is of the utmost importance and that voters are convinced, also tricked, by convincing rhetorical strategies. Richard Milhous Nixon won the presidential race, and his presidency lasted from January 20, 1969 to August 9, 1974. *Miami and the Siege of Chicago* is therefore a significant work because it depicts the misuse of rhetoric for political purposes during a tumultuous era in American politics and society.

Mailer's attitude towards young people changed by the time *Miami and the Siege of Chicago* was published. He no longer has confidence in the "Hippies" and "Yippies".

Wenke also discussed Mailer's attitude towards the American youth. He states that "focusing on the hippies and Yippies in Lincoln Park, Mailer repeatedly refers to the demonstrators as "children" or 'kids'…from Mailer's point of view the hippies' radically democratic vision of life leads to an elimination of meaning through the denial of all distinctions" (172).

Mailer's views give the impression that he does not believe in the bright future of America because he does not have faith in the nation's young people. This position is perfectly legitimate, but is based on the unusual arguments accusing American youth of their naiveté. Perhaps the writer took such a standpoint towards young people in order to emphasize that the country was on the wrong path, a path that would not lead to a better future for all.

Another important topic Mailer discusses in the novel is the war in Vietnam. He is very critical towards the war, he considers so unfair that even God decides to cheer for America's enemies:

> No matter what excuse was given that there might have been better ways to wage the war, the Wasp had built his nest with statistics, and the figures on the Vietnam war were badly wrong. How could the nation fail to win when its strength was as five to one, unless God had decided that America was not just? – righteousness had taken a cruel crack on the bridge of its marble brow. (Mailer, Miami 60)

For Mailer, the decision to fight the war in Vietnam was a terrible one and he often emphasizes that:

> "As we look at America we see cities enveloped in smoke and flame. We hear sirens in the night. We see Americans dying on distant battlefields abroad. We see Americans hating each other, fighting each other, killing each other at home. ... Did we come all this way for this? ... did in Normandy and Korea and Valley Forge for this? Listen to the answers[.]" (Mailer, Miami 76)

According to Mailer, the United States fights wars in foreign countries not out of principle, but are instead driving bythe greed of certain powerful individuals and political corruption:

> The moral powers of the vegeterian, the pacifist, and the nationalist have been so refined away from the source of much power – infantile violence – that their moral powers exhibit a leanness, a keenness, and total ferocity which can only hint at worlds given up: precisely those sensuous worlds of corruption, promiscuity, fingers in the take, political alliances forged by the fires of booze, and that sense of property which is the fundament of all political relations. (Mailer, Miami 89)

All this leads to totalitarianism, another theme that accompanies Mailer throughout his ouvre. Because Mailer understands totalitarianism as a form not limited only to authoritarian governments and leaders such as Hitler, Mussolini and Stalin, Mailer suggests that because of its many bad decisions and the war in Vietnam, American policy has taken on some characteristics of totalitarianism.

Mailer believes that the appeal for peace was often just empty words. In his 1968 speech, the Republican Nixon stressed the need to end the war in Vietnam with honor (76). The Democrat Humphrey called for peace (204). Mailer, on the other hand, apparently resisted both rhetorical strategies:

> Then he (Humphrey) called for peace in Vietnam, and the crowd roared and the band played Dianas as if he had made a glorious pass. Peace in Vietnam was now the property of all politicians; peace in Vietnam was the girl who had gone to bed with a thousand different guys, but always took a bath, and so was virgin. Hubert felt like a virgin every time he talked of peace in Vietnam. (Mailer, Miami 204)

The war in Vietnam ended in 1975. Mailer despised presidential rhetoric and also the electoral machine, so it perhaps comes as no surprise when it is stated that "Norman Mailer would probably not vote" (217).

Mailer also portrays himself as a patriot in *Miami and the Siege of Chicago*, and speaks of American cities with enthusiasm:

> Chicago is the great American city. New York is one of the capitals of the world and Los Angeles is a constellation of plastic, San Francisco is a lady, Boston has become Urban Renewal, Philadelphia and Baltimore and Washington blink like dull diamonds in the smog of Eastern Megalopolis, and New Orleans is unremarkable past the French Quarter. Detroit is a one-trade town, Pittsburgh has lost its golden triangle. St Louis has become the golden arch of the corporation, and nights in Kansas City close early. The oil depletion allowance makes Houston and Dallas naught but checkerboards for this sort of game. But Chicago is a great American city. Perhaps it is the last of the great American cities. (Mailer, Miami 83)

Mailer's patriotism can also be seen through his references to American literature in which he mentions John Updike and Theodor Dreiser (*Miami* 15, 84).

The message of the book can be summed up in the following observation from the novel: "Freedom does not work unless we work at it," he said, "and that I believe to be part of the reason for the spirit and determination of so many of the young people" (Mailer 200).

3.7.3 Why Are We in Vietnam?

The plot of the novel *Why Are We In Vietnam?* is about a group of hunters from Texas who went to Alaska on an organized bear hunting trip. The book was first published in 1967. Much later, in his book on writing *The spooky Art* Mailer commented on his work as follows:

> *Why Are We In Vietnam?* is the only novel I ever finished under the mistaken belief I was writing another. /.../ I imagined a group of seven or eight bikers, hippies and studs plus a girl or two, living in the scrub thickets that sat in some of the valleys between the dunes. Only six feet high, those thickets were nonetheless forests, and if you could find a path through the thorns and cat briars, nobody

could track you, not in a hurry. So I peopled the thickets with characters: My characters were as wild as anyone who ever came to Provincetown. /.../ I began the book in the spring of '66. It attracted me too much not to begin. Yet because I could not thrust Provincetown into such literary horrors without preparation, I thought I would start with a chapter about hunting bear in Alaska. A prelude. I would have two tough rich boys, each as separated from social convention as any two rich boys could be – Texans I would make them, out of reserve memories of Texans I had served with in the 112th Cavalry out of San Antonio. The boys would still be young, still mean rather than uncontrollably murderous – the hunting might serve as a bridge to get them ready for more. They would come back from the Alaskan hunting trip ready to travel; Provincetown would eventually receive them. (Mailer, Spooky 233–234)

The reader realizes that nobody comes to Provincetown. Hunting in Alaska serves as a metaphor for the war in Vietnam. According to Wenke in his analysis of the Alaskan hunting trip, and its cultural, political and psychological implications, which together come to represent the character of the United States and provide "the thematic context for the novel's explanation of America's involvement in Vietnam" (126). In the book, hunting is presented in a negative light, and Mailer calls the United States of America "all the United Greedies of America" (206). Hunting tourism is only one aspect of that greed. In response to the title question, the word 'Vietnam' actually occurs only twice in the novel, so the answer to the question must be uncovered in the allegory of the story depicted in the novel.

The story is about hunters who have a guide in the organized hunting and therefore they have a great advantage over the bears. What is more, the guide is also responsible for their safety, even with the help of a helicopter, which disables the dignified struggle between man and beast. In the novel, the harmful presence of technology in the wilderness is embodied by the guide's assistant Ollie: "Brooks Range no wilderness now. Airplane go over the head, animal no wild no more, now crazy" (65). Further on, a guide named Luke is described:

> *The helicopter was new to him, you read, and for some parties in the last year or so he'd begun to use it, for some not, but he was an American, what the fuck, he had spent his life living up tight with wilderness and that had eaten at him, wilderness was tasty but boredom was his corruption, he had wanted a jolt, so sees it D.J., Big Luke now got his kicks with the helicopter. He was forever enough of a pro not to use it with real hunters, no, man, but he had us, gaggle of goose fat and asshole, killers of bile-soaked venison, so the rest of the hunt, all next seven*

> *days he gave what was secretly wanted, which was helicopter heaven /.../ (Mailer, Vietnam 98-99)*

D. J. is punished for his unfairness and he also pays the moral price for it. When he shoots the mountain goat with the single shot, his first catch in Alaska, he is moved by his act:

> */.../ animal stood on its nose for one long beast of a second, and then did a running dying dance for fifty yards down the rocks like a fakir sprinting through flaming coals, and when he died, Wham! the pain of his exploding heart shot like an arrow into D.J.'s heart, and the animals had gotten him, they were talking all around him now, communicating the unspoken unseen unmeasurable electromagnetism and wave of all the psychic circuits of all the wild of Alaska, and he was only part of them, and part he was of gasoline of Texas, the asshole sulfur smell of money-oil clinging to the helicopter /.../ (Mailer, Vietnam 99-100)*

Mailer uses vulgar language, rhymes, the stream of consciousness technique, and unusual punctuation. He employs these varied stylistic features to carry out his experiment of demonstrating violence and various excesses in a literary way. Mailer's message is anti-war.

At the end of the book, D.J. is at a farewell party before going to Vietnam, and the novel concludes with the following excerpt:

> */.../ Rusty and Luke and the guides and boys and packers and medium assholes all got into the planes to go on back to Fairbanks and led the way into the new life smack right up here two years later in my consciousness, D.J. here at this grope dinner in the Dallas ass manse, given in my honor, D.J., I thank you, because tomorrow Tex and me, we're off to see the wizard in Vietnam. Unless, that is, I'm a black-ass cripple Spade and sending from Harlem. You never know. You never know what vision has been humping you through the night. So, ass-head America contemplate your butt. Which D.J. white or black could possibly be worse of a genius if Harlem or Dallas is guiding the other, and who knows which? This is D.J., Disc Jockey to America turning off. Vietnam, hot damn. (Mailer, Vietnam 207-208)*

The ending of the novel *Why Are We In Vietnam?* is particulary rich for interpretation; as Wenke (136) points out, the critics Tony Tanner, Adams, Merrill, and Aldridge all offer different opinions on the ending. Wenke points to the issue of "identifying the ethical significance of the boys' mystical encounter with a deadly yet divine force in nature and relating the lesson to their subsequent enthusiasm over the immediate prospect of fighting in Vietnam" (136-137), and also argues that "one realizes too that with this novel, Mailer pressed his advocacy of violent left radicalism to its limit" (138). However, it should be remembered that, as Lewallen points out, this is a decidedly anti-war book (2014: 320).

3.7.4 Of a fire on the Moon

Of A Fire On the Moon (1970) is an extensive nonfiction novel and the work for which the author calls himself "a true journalist" (413), despite the fact that he considers himself a writer rather than a journalist. In his personal life, he even considered calling himself a journalist to be offensive: "While Aquarius had never been accorded the respect he thought he deserved as a novelist, he had been granted in compensation the highest praise as a journalist" (11). In the novel, Mailer plays a role of the romantic poet Aquarius (Mailer's astrological sign) who contemplates on the universe as "the key to our future on earth" (73). In the book, Mailer also indicates that the loss of the ego is a prerequisite for the emergence of a high-quality literary work – a very challenging task he imposes on himself:

> So Aquarius began to live without his ego, a modest quiet observer who went on trips through the Space Center and took in interviews, and read pieces of literature connected to the subject and spent lonely nights not drinking in his air-conditioned motel room, and thought – not of himself but of the size of the feat and the project before him, and by the night before the launch, he was already in orbit himself, a simple fellow with a mind which idled agreeably, his mind indeed out in some weightless trip through the vacuum of a psychic space, for a mind without ego he was discovering is kin to a body without gravity. He was there now merely to observe, to witness. And the days went quietly by. We would pick him up on the night before the launch, but we may not be able to. He is beginning to observe as if he were invisible. A danger sign. Only the very best and worst novelists can write as if they are invisible. (Mailer, Fire 56)

Mailer's mission to attain a kind of ego death ended relatively successfully. It was perhaps only a partial victory, because in the final section of the novel, Mailer gets more involved in the plot by making reflections on a decaying marriage and his own life, which render him something more than a mere observer, invisibly present in the novel, as was his stated aim.

Mailer's *Of A Fire on the Moon* is not only an extensive, but multilayered work on the Apollo moon landing in 1969. It is a metaphorical and stylistically rich description of the adventure by the author described "as a product finally of the twenty-four billion dollars spent, and ten years of concerted effort, and mishaps beyond number" (167), which he depicts as a result of hard teamwork in stressful situations, political lobbying and the corruption of large corporations. The book offers insight into the lives of astronauts and their physical and mental qualities, explains the structure of NASA and the history of the flights. Space technology is discussed precisely and in scientific terms. With this novel, Mailer demonstrates that science is not at odds with literature, and can be used to inspire a masterful literary work: "It was a terror to write if one wished to speak of important matters and did not know if one was qualified" (396). The writer tries to adjust to the world in which technology prevails over nature.

The novel depicts the Apollo journey to the Moon, an event which gives occasion for Mailer to voyage into his innerself. In this work, Mailer as an artist confronts with the world of technology and science. There are two opposite poles in the novel: Aquarius and NASA, poetry and science, God and satan, good and bad. Aquarius as a poet is confronted with the world of technology, which brings progress, but also has certain drawbacks. Similarly, Kernan points out that at the heart of the novel is "a confrontation of the poet with science" (19), meaning that poetry and literature represent certain standpoints, values and the attitudes towards the world:

> Literature, or art in general, is not, Of A Fire on the Moon reveals, some unchanging, immutable thing, some eternally privileged way of writing about reality whose authority is located in some perennial psychological power – genius, imagination, sensitivity – or in some especially true way of writing – fiction, plot, hero, character, organic form – or in some special form of language – verse, metaphor, symbol. It is rather the expression of a set of values, a humanistic way of looking at and understanding the world, which has selected and stressed, made the essence of poetry, those ways of thinking and writing that, among all the many possibilities available, express its values and satisfy its needs /.../ (Kernan 31)

Art deserves a special place in the world, according to Mailer:

> To worship science was like being married to a beautiful woman who furnished your castle, bore your children, decorated and illuminated your life, filled your days, was indispensable. Yet all the while you did not know the first thing about her true nature. Was she in love with you or a masterpiece of hate? There, in the centre of the dream, was not an answer but an enigma. Was light corpuscular or a wave? Or both. Both! (Mailer, Fire 154)

Acccordingly, Aquarius needs to fight for a suitable position of poetry in society, as science and technology are in the forefront of the book.

As Mailer himself stated in an interview with Leeds, he was very depressed when writing *Of a Fire on the Moon* (Leeds 122–123). The tone of the book is pessimistic, but nevertheless, the book is still topical nowadays, and if the style, topics and messages are observed, *Of a Fire on the Moon* is among Mailer's most outstanding works in the 1970s.

As in his previous works, he also approached this novel with the utmost care as a patriotic citizen of the United States. Even though he finished his engeneering studies at Harvard and he was well versed in science, he was skeptical about whether he would be competent enough in the subject to write this book (Mailer 152). His goal was to show what was wrong in the society with the goal of making it less corrupt and more fair. He writes a lot about the United States of America and is very worried about the future of his home country. In this novel, he refers to the society of the United States "Computersville":

> Computersville had no cure for skin disease but filth in the wound, and the guru had no remedy for insomnia but a trip to the moon, so people would be for ever migrating between the societies. Sex would be a new form of currency in both worlds – on that you could count. The planner and the swinger were the necessary extremes of the computer city, and both would meet in the orgies of the suburbs. (Mailer, Fire 133)

NASA's flight to the moon was only a matter of time. It had to happen at any cost before entering the 1970s:

> Somewhere in the centre of NASA was the American disease: focus on one problem to the exclusion of every other. When Communism had been the problem, then nothing had existed for national policy but anti-Communism. Now, ever since the fire of Apollo 204, there had been only one idea at NASA. Get men to the moon by the end of the decade and get them back. If drama had to be sacrificed, rid the situation of drama. If scientific investigations would hamper a smooth flight, restrict scientific investigation. A narrowness of vision, constricted by the panic which followed the Apollo fire, lost all register of the true complexity of the event /.../. (Mailer, Fire 353)

When Mailer observed the many Americans who put up their tents at Cape Canaveral to watch the launch, he was critical of the fact that his fellow Americans could easily be made enthusiastic about new things and also manipulated by media, what is more, they were inclined to sensation and to everything new without a trace of sober reflection. Mailer was also concerned that with the landing of the Apollo on the moon, science would in effect 'kidnap' the Moon, taking over the ancient poetic symbol of longing and turn it into cold, plain scientific fact.

And behind this kidnapping of the Moon stands none other than NASA, an institution that Mailer compares to Nazism (Mailer, *Fire* 77):

> NASA. *The word had derived from NACA – National Advisory Committee for Aeronautics, which became the National Aeronautics and Space Administration, or NASA. It was an unhappy sound. Just think of NASA-ism. NASA would have no deliberate relation whatsoever to Nazi. But we are not a schizophrenic land for nothing. /.../ Aquarius was still brooding about Nazism. For the philosophy of the Folk, detesting civilization, claiming to be in love with the primitive, had nonetheless killed millions of men in the most orderly technological fashion yet devised. Nazism had been not one philosophy, but two – and each philosophy was utterly opposed to the other. It was primitive, it was vertiginously advanced. It gave brave men a sense of nobility in their hearts – it had been utterly heartless. It spoke of clean futures and buried Germany (for a time!) in vomit and slime and swill. /.../ Nazism had been an assault upon the cosmos – why think of it less? That is why it moved as the spectre behind every civilized transaction. For it had said: civilization will stifle man unless man is delivered on to a new plane. Was space its amputated limb, its philosophy in orbit?* (Mailer, Fire 77)

This radical comparison is an example of Mailer's habit of bringing his comparisons to the extreme. He does draw some political observations about NASA, namely that its space program is ideological and effectively moved the Cold War moved into space:

> Mailer emphasizes the dark sides of consumerism, the unfair and fraudulent company, as American has become according to Mailer, who believes that everything which hides a great idea could be sold to the Americans (Mailer, Fire 74–75).

Although Mailer somehow despises technology, he is not indifferent to the Apollo's flight. On the one hand, he is inspired by this technological breakthrough and he believes that the flight is a heroic act. However, on the other hand, he fears that man will become completely separated from nature and from the values associated with a romantic conception of the world. What is the price of technological progress? Will it destroy nature? Mailer suspects that the answer to this question is affirmative (Mailer, *Fire* 79).

Mailer comes to the conclusion that America is "An empty country filled with wonders" (97), where corporative capitalism is the generator of everything, up to and including the moon landing. In order to demonstrate the seriousness of the circumstances in the United States of America, he often uses hyperbole, making exaggerated statements such as calling a household computer "a diabolical machine." But even Mailer himself is often divided. On the one hand, he states that the computer is satan's work, and on the other that the computer is also "the greatest instrument ever handed to man" (322). Mailer exaggerates, again, probably to picture the dualistic nature of the world.

A great deal of the novel is devoted to reflecting on the future of the planet. Mailer fears for the future of the natural world because increasing technological progress results in the destruction or transformation of more and more nature. *Of a Fire on the Moon* can therefore also be thought of as an ecological novel, and unfortunately, also prophetic. During the summer of 1969, Mailer had a premonition of the ending, both about the end of the century, an era, "fin de siècle" (396), which ended with the landing on the moon, and finally, the ending of his marriage to Beverly Bentley and of many other marriages in Provincetown. Mailer's ominous feelings about the self-destruction of mankind for the price of progress seem to be founded.

Even though Mailer holds a standpoint of a romantic poet, often pessimistic, he also admires the astronauts Neil Armstrong, Edwin Buzz Aldrin and Michael Collins: "They were patriots, but they were moonmen. They lived with absolute lack of privacy, their obvious pleasure was to be alone in the sky. They were sufficiently selfless to be prepared to die for their mission, their team, their corporate NASA, their nation; yet they were willynilly narcissistic as movie stars" (Mailer, *Fire* 47).

The author goes further, and states that using your own brain in the civil and public services, such as NASA, is risky: "little could damage a man more than to be considered sympathetic to peace in Vietnam while working in Houston" (310). Mailer recognizes Aldrin's tribute to Martin Luther King in 1968 in Houston as a courageous political act. Another topic that Mailer could not avoid in his exploration of the space program is the Vietnam war. He speaks of the lack of patriotism in the United States (Mailer 313), and is from the beginning to the ending of the book aware of the fact that technology in the twentieth century was often used against humanity, and not to further develop humankind or human societies. For this reason, he emphasizes that the twentieth century was a period of great contrasts. The anxiety caused by the unprecedented development of technology is also typical for this period.

Despite the author's concerns regarding technological progress, his distrust towards technology and disappointment with it due to the many consequences and the price humanity has at times paid for this 'progress," Mailer does ultimately end his novel *Of A Fire On the Moon* by reconciling himself with progress.

Leeds argues that in *Of a Fire on the Moon* Mailer is forced to confront the possibility that "technology-oriented people of the establishment may, finally, have won the moon because in their dogged, unimaginative way they have earned the right to, while artists, intellectuals, and dropouts have submerged themselves in a lifestyle which has a sterility of its own" (27).

Thus, with the Apollo landing on the moon, the myth about science was finally enthroned. Not only that science overtook the name of a God to name the spacecraft, and conquered the greatest poetic symbol, but it also outlined the future, in a way, science symbolically conquered the future. Despite the romantic notion of the poet Aquarius, who acts as a representative of a minority culture – of those who are skeptical and capable of critical reflection in the novel, there is no way back. After the landing on the Moon, the world would never be the same again. The path towards space imperialism was finally opened.

Given the fact that violence is one of Mailer's leitmotifs, it should be noted that the violence in *Of a Fire on the Moon* is distinctly reflected in the dominance of the majority over the minority, technology over nature (and man), science over the arts, and in American capitalist organization – corporations and their money dictate the discovery and colonization of the universe and reign over the average person. Or as Dickstein stated: "Mailer feels betrayed by the gap between his romantic expectations and the gray but immense realities" (Dickstein, *New York Times*).

3.7.5 Why Are We at War?

Mailer's short collection of essays *Why Are We At War?* (2003) is a sharp critic of George W. Bush and his administration. The essays are accompanied by a Mailer interview by Dotson Rader. As in his previous works, Mailer stays loyal to his critical views and beliefs in this collection. Again, Mailer renders sharp criticism of the United States and American society, he is here even more ruthless and clearly articulated than in his earlier works.

Mailer states in the preface that he would never have published this book without the fatal events of September 11th. In addition to exploring the terrorist acts and the resulting invasions of Afghanistan and Iraq, Mailer contemplates U.S. patriotism, terrorism, corporate capitalism, the hatred of Muslims to westerners, Christianity, Bush's policy and his abuse of the word 'evil', technology etc. He even states that American capitalism, which is powered by technology and founded on a striving for power, threatens human existence: "Until the Left and that part of the Right that is still loyal to it sold values can come to recognize that no matter their essential differences, they also share one profound value they might look to protect in common – the vulnerable dignity of the human creation" (Mailer 103).

In *Why Are We at War?* Mailer revisits the major themes that appear from his first published novel, *The Naked and the Dead*. *Why Are We at War?* effectively contains all of the themes Mailer explored throughout his career in one place. Mailer's views on the issues of patriotism, terrorism, capitalism, totalitarianism and the attitude of the United States towards the rest of the world are expressed very clearly and unambiguously. The work is important because it reveals Mailer's views on the United States at the beginning of the new millennium and current American policy.

In the introduction of the book, there is a conversation that took place between Mailer and his friend Dotson Rader in which they discuss their experiences of September 11, 2001. The whole first part of the book is in the form of an interview, which was adapted from the London *Sunday Times Magazine* and was originally published a year after the fall of the Twin Towers.

Patriotism is again on Mailer's mind:

> *A mass identity crisis for all of America descended upon us after 9/11, and our response was wholly comprehensible. We were plunged into a fever of patriotism. If our long-term comfortable and complacent sense that America was just the greatest country ever had been brought into doubt, the instinctive reflex was to reaffirm ourselves. We had to overcome the identity crisis – hell, overpower it, wave a flag. (Mailer, War 12)*

Mailer continues: "We don't need compulsive, self-serving patriotism. It's odious. When you have a great country, it's your duty to be critical of it so it can become even greater. But culturally, emotionally, we are growing more arrogant, more vain. We're losing a sense of beauty not only of democracy but also of its peril" (Mailer, *War* 15–16). Uncritical patriotism is therefore very damaging, and good government should enable citizens (Americans in this case) to discuss and assess the policies and circumstances in the country soberly, without being blinded with mislead enthusiasm for their country.

Mailer clearly states that the fact that the country was once a great democracy does not guarantee that it will forever be a great democracy: "Democracy is existential. It changes. It changes all the time. That's one reason why I detest promiscuous patriotism. You don't take democracy for granted. It is always in peril" (ibid.).

In the text, Mailer deals extensively with the issues of terrorism and Muslim fundamentalism. To explain the hatred of Muslim fundamentalists towards white Americans, he argues that these people have a certain degree of envy towards those Americans they hate. Of course, there are also other, more uncomfortable reasons for the hatred, such as the threat of corporate capitalism dominating the economies of foreign countries. And according to Mailer, Americans themselves can also be partially to blame for frequently acting without cultural sensitivity who perhaps do not pay much attention to what – or who– is being trampled upon. This jealousy and anger is increased due to the economic and material success of the United States compared to many other parts of the world. At the core of the hatred Muslim fundamentalists feel towards the Americans is the fear that Muslims will lose their culture and religion due to the dominance of Western values and ways of life. As Mailer speculates, perhaps half of the people who live in Islamic countries secretly want to get rid of Islam, but on the other hand, those who want to maintain the old religion begin to response in extreme ways (Mailer 26). In his critique of the Islamic religion, Mailer emphasizes the concept of equality before god:

> *There is one fascinating element in Islam, which is the idea that all Muslims are equal before God, a tremendous egalitarian concept. Like all organized religion, Islam ends up being the perversion of itself in practice. Just as in Christianity, compassion is supposed to be the greatest good, but its present exercise in the world seems to be a study in military power and greed. In Islam, no Muslim has the right to consider himself superior to another Muslim. What happens in reality is that you have oppressive societies run for the wealthy, with the poor getting less and less – tremendous economic inequalities in many a Muslim society. And tyrannnical people in the seats of power. (Mailer, War 26–27)*

According to Mailer, the existing gap between Western and Islamic civilizations cannot be easily bridged.

The writer does not avoid the historical memory, and points out that some unpleasant facts from the past are easily forgotten. He reminds the reader that the major problems in the United States began with the dropping of the nuclear bombs, and that nuclear arms race had a great impact global humanity, a much greater impact, in fact, than September 11th. Humanity has never recovered from the awareness that the Earth is now effectively chained to a huge bomb capable of complete destruction. Mailer points out that the price the humanity pays since the first explosion of nuclear bombs has been enormous (Mailer 31).

In the second part of this collection, Mailer also cites some other literary but also politically active authors, among them John le Carré and Harold Pinter. Carré commented on the Iraq war in *The Times:* "America has entered one of its periods of historic madness, but this is the worst I can remember." And Pinter observed: "The American administration is now a bloodthirsty wild animal. Bombs are its only vocabulary. Many Americans, we know, are horrified by the posture of their government, but seem to be helpless" (43).

Mailer goes on to argue that the United States entered the war with Iraq in order to establish a very large military presence in the Middle East, which would be a springboard for the conquest of the rest of the world, and the author also believes that Americans were experiencing the war with a certain degree of distance and irreality, as if it were only a television program (51).

Directly, and without hesitation, Mailer states that the war with Iraq will satisfy the need of the United States of America to avenge September 11th: " ... a war with Iraq will gratify our need to avenge September 11. It does not matter that Iraq is not the culprit. /.../ Saddam, for all his crimes, did not have a hand in September 11, but President Bush is a philosopher. September 11 was evil, Saddam is evil, all evil is connected. Ergo, Iraq" (Mailer, *War* 55).

Mailer also comments on the attitude of the United States of America towards Israel in this collection, and on the apparent policy priority to maintain good relations with Ariel Sharon, the Israeli Prime Minister during the period 2001–2006:

> *Protection of Israel is okay to Bush, electorally speaking, but it is also obligatory, especially when he cannot count on giving orders to Sharon that will always be obeyed. Sharon, after all, has one firm hold on Bush. With the Mossad, Sharon has the finest intelligence service in the Middle East if not in the world. The CIA, renowned by now for its paucity of Arab spies in the Muslim world, cannot afford to do without Sharon's services. (Mailer, War 55)*

When Mailer was preparing *Why Are We at War?*, the United States was at the height of the war against terrorism. Mailer believes terrorism to be of even greater evil than war:

> *The wars we have known until this era, no matter how horrible, could offer at least the knowledge that they would come to an end. Terrorism, however, is not attracted to negotiation. Rather, it would insist on no termination short of victory. Since the terrorist cannot triumph, he cannot cease being a terrorist. They are a true enemy, far more basic, indeed, than Third World countries with nuclear capability that invariably appear on the scene prepared to live with deterence and its in-built outcome – agreements after years or decades of passive confrontation and hard bargaining. (Mailer, War 66)*

He continues: "Terrorism can proliferate. It is not that complicated to be an effective terrorist, after all. Pick up the phone, make a call, and disrupt traffic for half a day. The real question is how pervasive can terrorism get, not whether you can wipe it out" (Mailer 84).

Mailer also discusses the forms of governance and outlines the characteristics of democracy, fascism and totalitarianism. From the time when *The Naked and the Dead* was published, the author constantly emphasized how fragile democracy really is: "Because democracy is noble, it is always endangered. Nobility, indeed, is always in danger. Democracy is perishable. I think the natural government for most people, given the uglier depths of human nature, is fascism. Fascism is more of a natural state than democracy" (Mailer 70). In his opinion, democracy is:

> *... the noblest form of government we have yet evolved, and we may as well begin to ask ourselves whether we are ready to suffer, even perish, for it rather than preparing ourselves to live in the lower existence of a monumental banana republic with a government always eager to cater to mega-corporations as they do their best to appropriate our thwarted dreams with their elephantiastical conceits. (Mailer, War 75)*

As in *Miami and the Siege of Chicago*, Mailer warns in *Why Are We at War?* that without effort, there can be no freedom, and sometimes fighting for freedom can not be avoided: "Freedom is as delicate as democracy. It has to be kept alive every day of our existence. So, yes, I do love this country. If our democracy is the noblest experiment in the history of civilization, it may also be the most singularly vulnerable one" (Mailer 110).

Economic crisis is another important topic of *Why Are We at War?*. Mailer warns about the seriousness of the economic and financial crises and the threats they can pose for democracy and peace:

> *If we have a depression or fall into desperate economic times, I don't know what's going to hold the country together. There's just too much anger here, too much ruptured vanity, too much shock, too much identity crisis. And, worst of all, too much patriotism. Patriotism in a country that's failing has a logical tendency to turn fascistic, just as too much sentimentality will corrupt compassion. Fascism in America is not going to come with a political party. Nor with black shirts or brown shirts. But there will be a curtailing of liberties. Homeland Security has put the machinery in place. The people who are running the county, in my opinion, simply do not have the character or wisdom to fight the concept of freedom if we suffer horrors; no, not if we suffer dirty bombs, terrorist attacks on a huge scale, virulent diseases. The notion that you're going to have your freedom saved by people who work for security agencies is curious at best. They're on a one-way street. Anything bad of that sort is very bad for them. So they're going to do their utmost to restrict the freedom of people during critical situations. In the final analysis, democracy is inimical to security. Americans have to be willing to say at a certain point that we're ready to take some terrorist hits without panicking, that freedom is more important to us than security. (Mailer, War 105–106)*

Curtailing the rights of citizens in the United States is very problematic to Mailer (105–108), as he details at length in *Why Are We at War?*. Safety, in his opinion, should not be more important than freedom. He also believes that fascism will not come to the country through the actions of a political party and their adherents, but by curtailing of human rights. *Why Are We at War?* reveals the atmosphere, the Zeitgeist of the early twenty-first century. Lewallen labels the book as a "simpler book" (2014: 320) and "a diagnostic work" (323), and adds that "in some ways perhaps things are simpler now: our politics have become more authoritarian, and less democratic" (ibid.). However, it also "makes the case in Mailer's sober style that democracy was and should remain the primary ideal and working aim of American culture" (Lewallen, 2014: 323).

3.8 The Swan Song – The Castle in the Forest

The Castle in the Forest (2007) is Mailer's last big novel, both in terms of its length and quality. It would be the eleventh, and the last of his books, to appear on the *New York Times* bestseller list. This last novel is about Adolph Hitler, and the majority of the novel is devoted to Hitler's childhood and his younger years. The German dictator fascinated Mailer, an interest which was already indicated in his first work, *The Naked and the Dead*. *The Castle in the Forest* is narrated by the devil, by satan himself: a member of the SS named Dieter. The novel begins with him introducing himself: "You may call me D.T. That is short for Dieter, a German name, and D.T. will do /.../" (Mailer, *Castle* 2). Dieter represents a supernatural power, a power that cannot be influenced. He was sent to guide Hitler to his destructive decisions.

Also this novel is a stylistic masterpiece. Mailer divides it into fourteen chapters that he calls books. At the beginning of the novel, America is labelled as "this curious nation" (Mailer, *Castle* 2). The whole novel is filled with "mailerisms," like this one, typical of his style. In the following description, for instance, he successfully combines the most primitive facts concerning the birth of a human being with sophisticated knowledge of Latin:

> During recess one morning, Adolf heard one of the students telling others about a medieval churchman, St. Odon, who was the Bishop of Cluny. "I have a brother who studies Latin," the boy said, "and he gave me my first lesson: 'Inter faeces et urinam nascimur.'" So soon as this was translated, Adolf was shocked, then thrilled. What strong language! True force! He was aroused enough to dare to go to the Anatomy Museum in Linz once school was out. He managed to get in by lying about his age and so was able to see a penis and a vagina, both modeled in wax, as well as a few fullsized naked men and women, also in wax. The Latin kept pulsing through his mind. To be born between piss and shit! That was what he had always supposed. Sex was filthy. (Mailer, Castle 443–444)

During his writing career Mailer returned to certain motives and phrases throughout his works, creating a kind of pattern. The phrase "*Inter faeces et urinam nascimur*" is used not only in *The Castle in the Forest*, but also in *The Naked and the Dead*. The soldiers in Mailer's first novel literally live this Latin phrase in the harsh conditions of the WW II in the Phillipines. Mailer's message is that despite progress and development average people can easily be defeated in their intentions and can find themselves "between shit and piss".

In *The Castle in the Forest*, Mailer vividly illustrates the consequences of societal violence on an individual. Family violence is one aspect that can contribute to a child becoming violent as an adult. Mailer provides an example of Hitler's father beating up young Adolph:

> *In later years, at the height of his power, Adolf Hitler would still believe that he had received a near-mortal beating. On many a night during the Second World War, at Headquarters in East Prussia for the Russian front, he would tell the tale to his secretaries as they sat at table after evening mess. He would be eloquent. "Of course, I deserved a whipping," he would say. "I gave real trouble to my father. My mother, I recall, was distraught. She loved me so, my dear mother." He would remember himself as being just as brave as Alois Junior, yes, he had stood up to his father. "I think that is why he had to beat me. I must have deserved it. I said terrible things to him, words so awful I cannot repeat them. Probably, I deserved this good beating. My father was a fine, strong, decent man, one Austrian who was a real German. Still, I do not know that a father should ever beat a son so close to death – it was a little too close." (Mailer, Castle 315–316)*

According to Mailer, violent individuals originate in violent families and societies. Despite the fact that *The Castle in the Forest is* not directly about America or Americans, it can also be seen as a critique of violence in American society, such as starting wars in foreign lands under the false pretenses of fighting for democracy and freedom.

4. Mailer's Reception in Europe and Slovenia

4.1 Translations

The works of Norman Mailer have been translated into several European languages, including: Croatian, Slovene, Serbian, Macedonian, Bulgarian, Polish, Czech, Slovakian, Italian, German, French, Spanish, Portuguese, Swedish, Hungarian, Greek, Norwegian, and Russian. His first novel, *The Naked and the Dead*, his most translated work, is according to Lennon, translated into at least 20 languages, including Chinese (2015). Ren Hujun states that a total of eight Mailer works have been translated into Chinese (2013: 119–133).

4.1.1 Mailer in Europe and The Balkans

Throughout Europe, Mailer is widely considered one of the most important American authors of the twentieth century, particularly in the former Republic of Yugoslavia. Mailer's popularity and critical reception in Europe cannot be explained only due to his good connections or, for example, that he was in Europe with his first wife studying at the Sorbonne in Paris when his first novel was published on May 6, 1948. *The Naked and the Dead* received excellent reviews also from European reviewers and was on the *New York Times* best-seller list from its publication until the summer of 1949, for a total of 62 weeks (Lennon 2013: 1–4).

According to *Cobiss.Net*, which is library information system of Serbia, Slovenia, Bosnia and Herzegovina, Macedonia, Montenegro, Bulgaria and Albania, and catalogues of national libraries of the former Yugoslav republics, Mailer's work had been translated into some European languages from early on in the author's career. In addition to Serbian and Croatian (translated by Magdalena Reljić, Tomislav Ladan, Nada Ćušić, Dušan Ćurčija, Antun Šoljan, Ivan Slamnig, Milica Babić, Branko Bucalo, Gordana Bunčić, Zlatko Crnković, Zoran Mutić, Stjepan A. Szabó etc., Milena Benini, Marko Maras) and Slovene (translated by Boris Verbič, Ana Padovan, Bojan Rambaher, Mira Mihelič), his works were also translated into the following European languages: Slovakian (translated by Rudolf Lesňák Junior, Šarlota Barániková, Viera Marušiaková, Ján Vilikovský etc.), Czech (Michael Žantovsky and others), Polish (Slawomir J. Magala and others), Macedonian (Kalina Janeva), Bulgarian (Todor Valchev), Italian (Vincenzo Mantovani, Pier Francesco Paolini, Bruno Tasso, Attilio Veraldi, Ettore Capriolo), German (Walter Kahnert, Johanna Thomsen, Matthias Büttner, Paul Baudisch, Dirk Muelder, Gisela Stege), French (Jean Malaquais, André Maurois, etc.), Spanish (Antonio Samons), Portuguese (José Manuel Calafate), Swedish (Clas Brunius), Hungarian (Szűr-Szabó Katalin, H. Prikler Renáta, Szijgyártó László, Matthias Büttner, Széky János, Gálvölgyi Judit, Szilágyi Tibor), Norwegian (Leo Strøm translated *The Naked and the Dead*, Hans-Olav Thyvold translated *The Executioner's Song* etc.), Greek (Politimi Gekas, several books, Mailer's last novel *The Castle in the Forest* among them), and Russian (Aleksandr Bogdanovsky, Olga Varshaver, Vladimir Babkov, Viktor Toporov, Tatiana Kudriavtseva, K. Soshinskaya, A. K. Slavanskaya etc., according to Peppard [2013: 109]). All the major works by Mailer have been translated into Russian, among them *The Naked and the Dead*, *The Deer Park*, *An American Dream*, *Tough Guys Don't Dance*, *The Executioner's Song* and *The Castle in the Forest*. Not all of the Mailer's translators could be located through library databases, the Internet, or in interviews. Because there are so many different translators, even Mailer's official biographer Lennon, who was interviewed via e-mail in 2015 on this topic, does not know the exact number of Mailer translations and translators.

4.1.2 Mailer in Croatian, Serbian, Macedonian and Slovene

After the Second World War, Serbia, Croatia, and Slovenia (until 1991 these countries were all part of the Socialist Federal Republic of Yugoslavia) were in relatively strong contact with contemporary American literature, at least with the works of the best and most popular authors from the United States, including Norman Mailer, whose novel *The Naked and the Dead* was translated into Croatian and Serbian in 1955 by Dušan Ćurčija, and into Slovene by Boris Verbič in 1958.

At the beginning of the 1950s, the post-war period in the reception of American literature in Yugoslavia began: more works of American authors were translated into Croatian, Serbian and Slovene, and a notable increase in the quality of the translations was observed. In the 1950s, Stanonik noted that foundations were laid "for all the subsequent work in the transfer of American literature to Slovenia" (332). This decade was crucial not only for Croatia, Serbia, Bosnia and Herzegovina, Montenegro and Macedonia, but also for all of Yugoslavia. The Serbian and Croatian languages (at the time called Serbo-Croatian) were intelligible by people of all Yugoslav nations and were the dominant languages in the region. For instance, the main television news called *Dnevnik* was aired in Serbian (or Serbo-Croatian).

In the years after the World War II, American influence in Serbia, Croatia, and Slovenia, but also in Bosnian Sarajevo, has grown continuously. With the American war novel, new names of the postwar generation of American authors were, to a vast extent, first introduced in Croatia, Serbia and Slovenia, among them Norman Mailer. Mailer's first novel *The Naked and the Dead* first became available to the Yugoslav public seven years after its initial publication in the United States. For the small Slovene nation (less than two millions inhabitants), it was published ten years after its American release, which seems quite late from today's perspective, but was relatively early at the time.

As early as the 1950s and 1960s, Zagreb, Croatia supported a series of translations of leading American authors, including Mailer. Due to official politics in Belgrade, which was the capital of Serbia and also the capital of the Socialist Federal Republic of Yugoslavia, and at the time the centre of decision making for the whole of Yugoslavia, encouraged (also by funding) the translations of certain American authors. In the period from the mid-1950s to mid-1960s, Yugoslavia was in the so-called 'golden decade.' The country was experiencing a period of economic development, technical innovations were introduced and various connections with the developed Western countries were established. In foreign affairs, forging connections with the United States of America was especially significant, and, therefore, the government sought to translate American authors. In fact, one of the goals of these measures was to familiarize Yugoslavs with American culture in the broadest sense. The publishing house Zora in Zagreb was one of the publishers that specialized in foreign titles in Croatia. The English Department of the Faculty of Arts in Zagreb already had American studies scholars. In Slovenia, the leading publishing houses after the Second World War were Mladinska knjiga and Državna založba Slovenije (both in Ljubljana, the capital). After the Second World War, the Faculty of Arts of the University of Ljubljana was also starting to develop English and American Studies, where the first lectures on American Literatures were held in 1961 by Slovene professor of English and American literature Janez Stanonik (Bucik et al. 2009: 23), who wrote that it was only "after the Second World War that we can say that Slovene translators effectively followed the contemporary developments in American poetry, prose, and drama" (Stanonik 329).

In addition to *The Naked and the Dead* (*Goli i mrtvi*, translated in 1955 by Dušan Ćurčija [lives in Serbia and Croatia], and published in Zagreb by Zora (it was also re-translated in 2003), the following Mailer's titles are available in Serbian and Croatian: *The Deer Park* (*Park jelena*, translated by Ivan Slamnig [1930–2001], published in 1958 in Zagreb by Zora), *An American Dream* (*Američki san*, translated by Antun Šoljan [1932–1993], published in Zagreb in 1967 by Matica Hrvatska), *Why are We in Vietnam?* (*Zašto smo u Vijetnamu?*, translated by Tomislav Ladan [1932–2008], published in Zagreb in 1969 by Naprijed), *The Armies of the Night* (*Vojske noći: povijest kao roman, roman kao povijest*, translated by Gordana Bunčić [lives in Croatia], published in Zagreb in 1971 by Zora), *Marilyn: A Biography* (*Marilyn: biografija*, translated by Branko Bucalo [1929—2015], published in Zagreb in 1974 by Prosvjeta), the essay *Genius and Lust* (*Genije i požuda*, translated by Zlatko Crnković [1931–2013], published in Zagreb in 1980 by Prosvjeta), *The Executioner's Song* (*Krvnikova pjesma 1*, *Krvnikova pjesma 2*, translated by Branko Bucalo [1929–2015], published in Zagreb in 1982 by Globus), *Tough Guys Don't Dance* (*Muškarčine ne plešu*, translated by Milica Babić [born 1956, lives in Sarajevo, Bosnia and Herzegovina], published in Sarajevo in 1986 by Svjetlost; in 2009 a new translation into Croatian was made by Milena Benini [1966] and published in Zagreb by Zagrebačka naklada), *Ancient Evenings* (*Drevne večeri 1*, *Drevne večeri 2*, translated by Zoran Mutić [1951, lives in Bosnia and Herzegovin], published in 1988 in Sarajevo and Ljubljana by Svjetlost), *The Gospel According to the Son* (*Evanđelje po sinu*, translated into Croatian by Stjepan A. Szabo [lives in Croatia], published by Izvori in Zagreb in 1997; and *Jevanđelje po Sinu Božjem*, translated into Serbian by Nada Ćušić [lives in Serbia], published in Belgrade in 1998 by Čigoja štampa), *The Castle in the Forest* (*Dvorac u šumi*, translated into Croatian by Saša Stančin [lives in Croatia], published by Vuković & Runjić in Zagreb in 2008; and *Zamak u šumi*, translated into Serbian by Magdalena Reljić [lives in Belgrade] and published in Belgrade in 2008 by Alnari).

Earlier Mailer's translations into Croatian and Serbian were prompt and of good quality, because the translators were men and women of letters, well-educated and often writers, critics or poets themselves. The difference between the Croatian and Serbian languages was often ignored (at the time, the language was called Serbo-Croatian, and was taught in primary schools all over Yugoslavia in addition to the mother tongues Slovenian in Slovenia and Macedonian in Macedonia, Serbo-Croatian was taught. Thus, Mailer was well known in Serbian, Croatian, and Bosnian literary worlds. Recent translations into Croatian, Serbian and Macedonian are of good quality as well, and from the point of today's reader, the language used in these translations is more fresh and modern, as some words used in the earlier translations have since fallen out of use. *The Naked and the Dead* was re-translated into Croatian in 2003 as *Goli i mrtvi* (the same title as in 1955) by Marko Maras (born in 1973). Alfa published the re-translated novel in Zagreb.

Following the Serbian and Croatian translations, Slovene translators began producing Slovene translations of the following Mailer's novels during the 1960s to 1980s: *An American Dream, The Executioner's Song* and *Tough Guys Don't Dance*. In total, today there are four of Mailer's novels available in Slovene translation: *The Naked and the Dead* (*Goli in mrtvi*, translated by Boris Verbič [1913–1984], Ljubljana: Državna založba Slovenije, 1958); *An American Dream* (*Ameriški sen*, translated by Mira Mihelič [1912–1985], Ljubljana: Mladinska knjiga, 1966); *The Executioner's Song* (*Krvnikova pesem*, translated by Ana Padovan [1941, lives in Slovenia], Koper: Lipa, 1982); and *Tough Guys Don't Dance* (*Nepremagljivi ne plešejo*, translated by Bojan Rambaher [lives in Slovenia], Maribor: Založba Obzorja, 1986). The total number of translations available is quite low, considering the popularity of Mailer's works. But on the other hand, this can also be seen as a respectful number, given that there are only two million speakers of Slovene and a number of Mailer's works were already available in Serbian and Croatian, both languages which are understood by the majority of people in Yugoslavia. However, it should be emphasized that the translations into Croatian, Serbian and Slovene were quite up to date and, more significantly, the quality of the translations is satisfying, and in many cases excellent. Mailer's fourth novel, *An American Dream* (1965) was translated into Slovene in 1966 by Mira Mihelič (1912–1985), who was the best translator of English at the time, and Antun Šoljan (1932–1993), also a writer himself, who translated this novel into Croatian and Serbian in 1967. Below are short excerpts from the original, in which Mailer calls the marriage of the protagonists Rojack and Deborah "a devil's contract" (1965/1969: 24), and the corresponding translations:

> Our marriage had been a war, a good eighteenth-century war, fought by many rules, most of them broken if the prize to be gained was bright enough, but we had developed the cheerful respect of one enemy general for another. So I had been able to admire the strategic splendor of leaving me in our apartment. It stifled her, she explained to me, it was a source of much misery. (Mailer, American 26)

> Naš je brak bio rat, primjer rata iz osamnaestog stoljeća, u kojem se protivnici bore s mnogim pravilima, iako većinu tih pravila krše, ako je nagrada, koje se time može steći, dovoljno privlačna, ali smo razvili vedro uzajmno poštovanje, kao jedan protivnički general prema drugom. Tako sam se mogao diviti njenoj strateškoj genijalnosti, kad me je ostavila u našem stanu. Objasnila mi je da je taj stan guši, da za nju predstavlja izvor tuge i muke. (Mailer, Američki san 26, transl. into Croatian and Serbian by Antun Šoljan)

> Najin zakon je bil vojna, dobra vojna iz osemnajstega stoletja, ki jo bojuješ po mnogih pravilih, vendar večino teh prelomiš, če je nagrada, ki si jo s tem lahko pridobiš, dovolj sijajna, toda začela sva gojiti drug do drugega vedro spoštovanje sovražnega generala do nekega drugega sovražnega generala. Torej sem lahko občudoval stratešku sijajno potezo, da me je pustila v najinem stanovanju. Duši jo, mi je pojasnila, zanjo je vir velike stiske. (Mailer, Ameriški sen 26, transl. into Slovene by Mira Mihelič)

Both translations of *An American Dream* are of good quality, but for a contemporary audience, the language is dated in certain parts. A translator today would probably use different words that are more standard usage, but the essence of Mailer's original meaning is retained both in Croatian/Serbian (Serbo-Croatian) and in Slovene. There are, of course, some linguistic dilemmas, which could be solved differently, one of them is also in the above excerpt (what stifled Deborah – the apartment or the marriage situation? Šoljan decided that it was the apartment, and Mihelič left this dilemma unresolved).

At a 2015 workshop held at the scientific summer school at the University of Zadar, Croatia, with eleven students and six teachers (professors, associate professors and assistants) of translation studies from Slovenia and Croatia, students and teachers were faced with a dilemma of how to translate the phrase "It stifled her." Attendees of the workshop were wondering what exactly *stifled her*: was it the apartment, the marriage or the situation as a whole, and had difficulties translating this part with this phrase. Mira Mihelič (who translated Mailer into Slovene, but her mother tongue is actually Croatian) decided to leave this dilemma unresolved, translating "It stifled her" as "*Duši jo,*" while Antun Šoljan translated it as "je taj stan guši." Both translators also changed the verbal tense of this sentence. Mailer used the past tense, while Mihelič and Šoljan used the present tense in Slovene and Croatian. Attendees of the workshop believed that Šoljan's decision in the Croatian translation was more suitable than Mihelič's translation into Slovene, but this evaluation is of subjective nature, however, when considering only professional arguments, both solutions are acceptable and correct because they do not change the essence of the original.

From today's point of view, Mihelič's translation of *An American Dream* into Slovene has become dated. These days, the title of the novel would more likely be translated as *Ameriške sanje* and not *Ameriški sen*. In the Slovene translation by Mihelič, there are also the following archaisms: odtistihdob (nowadays: takrat, od takrat), e. g. "Odtistihdob sem, kakor pravim, romal gor in gotovo tudi dol in potem še gor in dol." (1966: 13); zdruzgan (nowadays: zmečkan, zdrobljen), e. g. "/.../ vzpela pet nadstropij visoko v stanovanjski hiši mimo sladkih zdruzganih gnijočih lesnih duhov kletnega skladišča za ceneno vino, gor po stopnicah /.../" (1966: 156); udje (nowadays: udi), e. g. "/.../ zid se mi je približal, moji udje so spet oživeli /.../" (1966: 333); nizdol (nowadays: navzdol), e. g. "Nato se le luč spremenila in ubrali smo pot po Lexingtonski avenji nizdol, dvaindvajset milj na uro mimo omahujočih luči." (1966: 335); drugekrati (nowadays: ob drugih priložnostih, drugikrat), e. g. "Drugekrati pa New York ponoči ni spal in to so bile noči za zver, nocoj je takšna noč." (1966: 336), etc.

Later, Branko Bucalo (1929–2015), who translated *The Executioner's Song* into Croatian and Serbian in 1982 along with many other literary works, and Ana Padovan (1941), who translated this Pulitzer Prize winning novel into Slovene in 1983, did an excellent job as well. They both were writers. Because of specific law vocabulary and non-existent English-Slovene and English-Croatian dictionaries in this professional area at the time, translating *The Executioner's Song* was particularly challenging. Below are the excerpts from the original and the corresponding translations into Croatian/Serbian and Slovene, which confirm the excellence of these translations. Again, however, the question of dated language arises:

> On the other hand, if he had been kept in jail in Idaho, Court would have had to refer him to the Oregon authorities, which is where his parole originated. It would have been difficult in the extreme to find any members of the Oregon Parole Commission on Sunday afternoon. In fact, it might even take a few days before they could meet to decide on Gilmore's violation. Gary would be sitting in a Twin Falls jail all that time. Right there, a lawyer could spring him on a Writ of Habeas Corpus, and Gilmore could take off. The more he was really in trouble, the more he'd look to get himself lost real fast, Whereas, Gilmore, coming back on his own, would be fortifying the positive side of himself. He would know Court had been right to trust him. That would give a base on which to work. The idea was to get a man into some kind of positive relationship with authority. Then he might begin to change. (Mailer 53)

> Res je, da bi moral Gilmora, če bi ga bili zadržali v zaporu v Idahu, Court prijaviti oregonskim oblastem, ker so ga pač tam pogojno izpustili. V nedeljo popoldne pa bi bilo neizmerno težko najti kakega člana oregonske komisije za pogojni izpust. Pravzaprav bi uteglo trajati nekaj dni, preden bi se komisija sestala in odločila glede Gilmorove kršitve. Medtem bi sedel Gary v zaporu v Twin Fallsu. Tožilec bi ga lahko že tam presenetil in zahteval, da se mora pojaviti pred sodiščem, in šele potem bi Gilmore lahko odšel. Bolj ko bi bil v škripcu, bolj bi se trudil, da čim hitreje izgine. Tako pa je zdaj Gilmore s tem, ko se je vrnil sam od sebe, okrepil svoj pozitivni jaz. Zavedal se je, da je imel Court prav, ko mu je zaupal. To je bila osnova za nadaljnje delo. Pomembno je pripraviti človeka tako daleč, da sprejme neki pozitivni odnos do oblasti. Tokrat se utegne spremeniti. (Mailer, transl. into Slovene by Padovan 67, *Krvnikova pesem*, 1st book)

> S druge strane, da ga je zadržao u zatvoru u Idahou, Court bi o njemu morao izvijestiti vlasti u Oregonu, odakle je potekao uvjetni otpust. Bilo bi sasvim teško naći i kojeg člana Oregonskog odbora za uvjetni otpust u nedjelju poslije podne. Zapravo je moglo proteći nekoliko dana prije nego što se odbor sastane i odluči u pogledu Gilmorove povrede otpusta. Cijelo to vrijeme Gary bi sjedio u zatvoru u Twin Fallsu. Uostalom, i tamo bi ga odvjetnik mogao izvaditi, podnoseći pismenu predstavku o mjesnoj nenadležnosti, pa bi Gilmore mogao dići sidro. Što više bude zaglavljen stvarnim teškoćama, što će više i brže poraditi na tome da se izgubi. S druge strane, ako se Gilmore vrati sam, to će značiti da učvršćuje pozitivnu stranu svoje ličnosti. Prokljuvit će da je Court imao pravo što mu je povjerovao. To bi stvorilo osnovu na kojoj bi se moglo raditi. Naime, čovjeka valja dovesti u neku vrstu pozitivnog odnosa s vlašću. Tad bi mogao početi, da se mijenja. (Mailer, transl. into Croatian/Serbian by Branko Bucalo, 64–65, *Krvnikova pjesma*, 1st book)

Rambaher's 1986 translation of *Tough Guys Don't Dance* is also interesting, not so much because of the dated language, but because of his translation of the word 'asshole,' which he translated as *ritna luknja*:

> Patty Lareine je imela takšen glas. Z ustnicami in zelo suhim martinijem (ki pa ga je, o tem ste lahko prepričani, neprestano imenovala marty seco) je znala počenjati prav vražje stvari. "Bil je gin," je ponavadi rekla z vsem hripavim navdušenjem svojega skoraj prepovedano pohotnega grla, "bil je takšen gin, da bi kar fental staro babo. Ja, ritna luknja," oh, na moč nežno bi te vključila v to roganje, kakor da bi se po božji milosti celo ti, ritna luknja, lahko prav prijetno počutil, če so te pota vodila do nje. (Rambaher, 1986: 21)

The translation *ritna luknja* is inaccurate. Nobody uses the swear word *ritna luknja* in Slovene. The appropriate translation would have been *kreten*, or a bit stronger *prasec*.

In 2013, Mailer's first novel *The Naked and the Dead* was also translated into Macedonian by Kalina Janeva under the title *Goli i mrtvi* and was published in Skopje by the publishing house Makavej. Kalina Janeva (1981) belongs to the younger generation of Macedonian translators. She graduated with a degree in English Language and Literature from the Faculty of Philology in Skopje, and where she lives. The fact that Mailer's first novel, *The Naked and the Dead*, was first published here in 2013 before even his later novels is an evidence that Norman Mailer is still relevant to contemporary audiences. Indeed, Mailer is now available to Macedonian audiences and can be put in the world literary canon.

4.1.3 Yugoslav Media on Mailer

The Yugoslav media reported on Mailer when his works were released in Yugoslav translations (Serbo-Croatian, Croatian, Serbian, Slovene), when his new novels were published in the United States, and every time he received a prestigious literary prize. The affairs and excesses of Mailer's private life and his political activism also repeatedly attracted the attention of Yugoslav media. However, in-depth assessments of Mailer's works or their translations into Slovene, Serbian or Croatian are rare, which is characteristic of the region's scholarly journals on literature and language.

In 1995, Slovene national newspaper *Delo*[2] published a translation of an interview with Mailer in which the author discussed his novel *Harlot's Ghost*, whose main heroine is the CIA. When asked why he decided to write about CIA, he responded:

> As a novelist, I have always dealt with the question of identity, the writer needs to know what are his foundations, and where from he is sending his messages. This issue has plagued me since my first novel, I have constantly researched myself, and this brings about the changes in habits, friends and the ways of life. On the other hand, I was always interested in spies, because they obviously have problems with dual identity, and for years I have been engaged in introspection, so to speak spy myself for me. The CIA is somehow a shadow of the government, its counterpart, its phantom and the hidden side, and yet, the side that knows best what is the purpose of a certain mission. It is also true that the world of espionage is an image, a reflection of some sort of prostitution (harlot also means a prostitute in English), which is widespread among famous people, actors, journalists: everyone is a prostitute in the sense of pretending that they are more satisfied with something than they really are. A journalist, for example, inevitably fascinates a person her or she interviews, because of giving him/her a feeling that he/she is special; when this person later reads the article, he/she is disappointed because he/she realizes that that journalist's opinion is different from what he/she expected. And journalism is a very subtle form of prostitution, much worse is with advertisements in which manufacturers exactly like prostitutes pretend to offer something out of love. An informant actually does not seek to pleasure the customer, he is trying to produce the most likely lie, cheat the enemies and try to find a traitor among them. Therefore, prostitutes are around him, and he plays more the role of a pimp.

Further on in this interview Mailer states:

> We are victims of plastic, commercials, television. No one has taken into account the horrors of capitalism. Communism brainwashed the Russians for seventy years, but it did not quite succeed because the Russians were too aware of it. It was too obvious – if you see huge banners with Lenin's thoughts along the road, you understand what's going on; but if you stare at television and are being bombarded with commercials, this is brainwashing that you are not aware of. The damage being produced is certainly bigger than that with the famous ozone hole, the damage are the holes in our souls.

It should be mentioned that Mailer also commented political circumstances in Yugoslavia, particularly Milosevic's regime:

---

2   "Vohuniti za samim seboj." *Delo*, 1 July 1995.

> *What may be more to the point is not Milosevic's personal pain, nor his wife's, but the identity he acquired as a young Communist in a Yugoslav regime at odds with Stalin but nonetheless profoundly influenced by the Soviet sense of virtue. The good Soviet operator was a dedicated bureaucrat who could climb the greasy pole of Party advancement skillfully enough to beat his fellow tigers. Milosevic had to be one of the wiliest, toughest, most treacherous, canny, tricky, ruthless, and resourceful human beings Madeleine Albright had ever encountered. (Mailer, Washington Post, May 1999)*

When in 2002 Mailer was awarded an important Austrian literary award, the Honorary Cross of Science and Art of the first order, *Delo*[3] published an article on Mailer and his views of contemporary American politics.

The Yugoslav media reported quite extensively on Mailer in 2003 when the writer celebrated his 80th birthday. In February 2003, when *The Spooky Art* was released, newspaper *Delo*[4] published a short interview with the author (translated from the American news magazine *Newsweek*). In the same month, *Delo*[5] also published Mailer's essay on democracy – again a translation, from the *International Herald Tribune*.

In May 2003, another Slovene national newspaper, *Dnevnik*[6], published an article by Croatian Professor Maroje Mihovilović, who described how Norman Mailer upset conservatives in the United States by analysing the Iraq war using Freudian methods. Mailer wrote that the United States opted for the war in Iraq so that the white American male could demonstrate his dominance. The famous writer also argued that this is precisely why Americans are continuing their military and political attacks on Syria, Saudi Arabia and Iran. In the article, Mihovilović also shortly introduced Mailer's life story and added that some of the worst criticism Mailer suffered was in response to his analyses of the Iraq war.

In 2003, Mailer's *Why Are We at War?* was published, and *Delo*[7] wrote about it under the title "Norman Mailer vs. George Bush." In May 2003, *Delo*[8] devoted another article to *Why Are We at War?*. The book was

---

3 "Norman Mailer odlikovan na Dunaju." *Delo*, 28 September 2002.
4 "Norman Mailer, pisatelj: To je eden naših velikih kulturnih proizvodov: drek." *Delo*, 7 February 2003.
5 "Dobili imperij, izgubili demokracijo." *Delo*, 28 February 2003.
6 "Esej o beli možatosti razburil konservativce." *Dnevnik*, 24 May 2003.
7 "Norman Mailer proti Georgeu W. Bushu." *Delo*, 5 June 2003.
8 "Zakaj je svet v vojni." *Delo*, 5 May 2004.

deemed important because it revisited the topics that had accompanied Mailer since the beginning of his career. The article by Branko Soban summarizes the content of the book and concludes with the following thought: "It would, therefore, be time to stop George W. Bush. The Americans are offered an opportunity for this in this year's presidential elections."

In January 2004, another Slovene national newspaper *Večer*[9] wrote on Mailer's warnings about the imperialistic tendencies of the United States of America. In 2004, *Nedelo*[10] published an article on the influence of the Mailer's *The Executioner's Song* on the prisoner Jack Abbott. The murderer, who was serving a life sentence in prison, wrote a letter to Mailer and offered himself to be his internal source from prison, which would be very helpful to Mailer, who was writing on Gary Gilmore. Mailer agreed and in the following months a lively correspondence developed between them.

In March 2005, Slovene cultural magazine *Ampak*[11] wrote about Mailer as a first to launch a form of the non-fictional novel that was a mixture of journalistic reporting on contemporary events, political commentary, critical provocations, autobiography, and novelistic fiction. This article appeared in response to the appearance of many translations of Mailer's *Portrait of Picasso as a Young Man* into European languages across Europe in 2005, although there was no translation into Slovene.

In 2005, for example, Yugoslav press agencies and *Slovenian Press Agency*[12] among others, reported that Mailer won the Honorary Award for Lifetime Achievement, which is awarded annually by the U. S. National Literary Foundation. The same news was also published in *Delo*[13], which stated that the rationale of the jury was as follows: "Mailer has long been an important figure in post-war American literature; with his inventive literary and non-literary works. He has changed American literature."

---

9 "Verjamem, da hudič obstaja in deluje." *Večer*, 10 January 2004.
10 "Pisatelj in njegova morilca. " *Nedelo*, 29 August 2004.
11 "Portret mladega Picassa." *Ampak*, 1 March 2005.
12 *"Prestiž za Normana Mailerja."* Slovenska tiskovna agencija, 20 September 2005.
13 "Nagrajen za življenjsko delo." *Delo*, 22. 9. 2005.

Mailer gained the attention of the most influential media in the former Yugoslavia again in 2007 when his novel *The Castle in the Forest* (in Croatian *Dvorac u šumi*, in Serbian *Zamak u šumi*, and in Slovene media translated as *Grad v gozdu*) was first published in the United Sates. Critics mostly asked themselves why Mailer decided to devote his novel to Hitler and the bloody history of the twentieth century. At the time, South African writer J.M. Coetzee's[14] reflective assessment of *The Castle in the Forest*, for example, was translated and broadcast on Channel 3 of National Radio Slovenia. And Serbian newspaper *Politika*[15] (www.webwm.com), for instance, stated that the dominant theme of the *Castle* is evil: "Ipak, glavna tema ovog romana jeste stalna Majlerova preokupacija: zlo kao neuništivi deo čovekovog bića."

Of course, the news of Mailer's death on November 10, 2007 was published in all the major media of the republics of the former Yugoslavia. His death occasioned the publication of many articles about his life and his works. Some cultural and political magazines, *Mladina*[16], for example, published obituaries. *Dnevnik*[17] and *Jutarnji list*[18] reported that Norman Mailer had been posthumously awarded the prize for the worst description of the sexual act, in his novel *The Castle in the Forest*.

The media in the former Yugoslavia still occasionally revisit Norman Mailer and his extraordinary works, such as when the Norman Mailer Award is granted or when the annual conference dedicated to Norman Mailer takes place in the United Sates. As a typical representative of literary journalism, Mailer is often used as a comparison to other authors, such as Truman Capote or the Swedish writer Per Olov Enquist (1934). In addition to this, the archives of National Radio and Television of Slovenia and Croatia hold some long and in-depth broadcasts on Norman Mailer.

---

14 Coetzee, J. M.: "Portret pošasti kot mladega umetnika: Recenzija romana Normana Mailerja Grad v gozdu." *Radio Slovenia*. 23 May 2007.
15 "Majlerova igra sa Đavolom." *Politika*, 31 March 2007.
16 "Beli črnec." *Mladina*, 2 December 2007.
17 "Pokojni Norman Mailer osvojil nagrado za najslabši opis seksa." *Dnevnik*, 29 November 2007.
18 "Norman Mailer: Dvorac u šumi." *Jutarnji list*, 2 December 2007.

4.1.4 Mailer is Still of Relevance in The Balkans

More than 25 years after the fall of the Berlin Wall, and almost as much after the dissolution of the Yugoslavian federation (Socialist Federal Republic of Yugoslavia fell apart in 1991), there are 21 books by Mailer available in the so-called Yugoslav languages, including different translations and retranslations. While Yugoslavia still existed, more of Mailer's books had been translated into the so-called Yugoslavian languages than after the dissolution of the Federation. Thus, one observation is that translations of Mailer's literature for Slovene, Croatian, Serbian, Bosnian, Macedonian, and Montenegrin readers could be more widely available. In the republics of the former Socialist Federal Republic of Yugoslavia, Norman Mailer is continuously being discovered. He was by all means known in the Yugoslav literary environment in the 1950s and 1960s, especially for his early-translated novels and some other successful works. One of the reasons that he was available to the literary audiences in Yugoslavia is that the authorities allowed his works to be translated and/or ordered to the leading publishing houses to translate some of his works. In the period after the Second World War, almost everything in Yugoslavia was directed and controlled by the state, including translations of foreign authors. It should be noted, however, that despite some of quite early translations of Mailer's works, scholars in Serbia, Croatia, Slovenia, Bosnia, Macedonia have yet to conduct in-depth analysis of his opus. But it is a significant fact, however, that in the former Socialist Federal Republic of Yugoslavia, the legacy of Norman Mailer continues through the translations, re-translations and re-evaluation of his works.

5. Mailer and Literary Tourism

5.1 Mailer – The Generator of Cultural and Literary Tourism

5.1.1 Literary Tourism

These days, the concept of literary tourism is well known, especially in the United States. Simply defined, literary tourism is a type of cultural or heritage tourism, primarily connected with authors and the settings of their works. By visiting the literary site, a visitor/tourist is able to better understand the author, his life and works more than by reading literary reviews. Some readers also visit places related to authors simply because they are inspired by the authors or their works. Literary pilgrims or literary tourists may be interested in how a place had influenced an author, or how a certain author or author's work created a place. Today, Provincetown, Massachusetts is probably most often associated to Norman Mailer.

According to Ghetau and Esanu (2001, witpress.com), working with specialised types of tourism promises an efficient approach toward the sustainable promotion of a destination. Literary tourism, as part of heritage tourism, is important in this respect (Perera, 2013) and recent research on literary tourism indicates a growing awareness that literature can be an important element in the structure and development of tourism, particularly in the sense that literary tourism has become a significant contributor to the local economy in many instances (Saunders, 2010 in Yiannakis & Davies, 2011: 1–2). Literature informs perceptions of visitors and their desire to visit certain places. Other literary destinations include places where a book was inspired or written, and the birthplaces or gravesites of deceased writers. For literary tourists, the author is the inspiration (Saunders, 2010, in Yiannakis & Davies, 2011: 2). In the case of Mailer, all of this holds true for Provincetown.

As Smith argues, "people enjoy stories because they give them pleasure" (2012: 24). Literary tourism thus represents an important kind of the heritage tourism, and literary tourists can be regarded "as a particular kind of heritage tourist" (Smith, 2012: 28). Smith also points out that in literary tourism "the customary process of reading leading to tourism ('text-to-tourism') can be inverted to an evolution of tourism leading to reading ('tourism-to-text')" (2012: 167). Recent research on literary tourism also indicates "a growing awareness that literature is an important element in the structure and development of tourism and the behaviour of tourists" (Saunders, 2010 in Yiannakis and Davies 2011: 1).

Shelagh Squire provides a shorter and perhaps more complete definition of this phenomenon by describing literary tourism as "travel to places famous for associations with books or authors" (1993: 5), and Nicola Watson believes that literary tourism is "interconnected practices of visiting and marking sites associated with writers and their work" (2009: 2). Thus, it could be claimed that literary tourism encompasses anything that is connected to literature, including literary events, performances and festivals. Yvonne Smith argues that also book signings and creative writing courses are parts of literary tourism (2012: 9). Her definition is therefore that literary tourism is "a form of cultural tourism involving travel to places and events associated with writers, writers' works, literary depictions and the writing of creative literature" (ibid.).

She (2012: 11) also remarks that not only prose, drama and poetry, but also biographies and autobiographies inspire people to become literary tourists. One of the earliest known examples of literary tourism is said to be connected to the writings of Petrarch in the south of Europe during the fifteenth century, and in the centuries that followed, literature continued to play an important role in both inspiring and shaping literary tours, mainly for the English elite (Es, 2015; Hendrix, 2009:15). Smith states that the earliest known practices of literary tourism can be traced to the ancient Roman world (2012: 59). Later, the classical Grand Tour focused on the antiquities of Italy, and did not include Greece or Spain (Löfgren, 2012: 342). The Grand Tour was primarily meant as an educational experience, including the pursuit of culture, pleasure and health (Adler, 1989; Towner, 2002 in Smith, 2012: 60; Towner, 1985: 297–333).

Ommundsen (2005) states that literary tourism is associated with many different activities, interests and locations, ranging from the sites that are physically associated with the lives of famous writers (houses, graves, statues, places where they studied, ate, drank, wrote, etc.) to events, tours and performances that commemorate the author and his or her works (2005). These sites may be marked by a commemorative plaque, or they may even be developed into complete tourist attractions, for example museums preserved or reconstructed to look exactly as they were at the writer's time that display collections of memorabilia such as personal relics, photographs, paintings, letters, manuscripts, and early editions. Some museums provide audiotapes and videos as well, including readings of the writer's work. Then there are events, tours, performances or commemorations (Ommundsen, 2005). Ommundsen also emphasizes festivals, which according to him have characteristics of their own in that they have "a tendency to confuse art and life and a desire to recreate the author as representative of and spokesperson for national, social or ethnic groups."

5.2 Legacy Power

Phillip Sipiora argues that the works of Norman Mailer, just like those of Fitzgerald or Hemingway, have "legacy power," meaning that they deserve to be passed on and preserved through the efforts of literary enthusiasts and academics (Lucas, 2013: 150). According to Lucas (*ibid.*), Mailer's legacy lives on in history and contemporary culture. In addition to that, there is a Norman Mailer archive in the Harry Ransom Center at the University of Texas at Austin, which in 2005 acquired the entire Mailer archive. According to Henderson et al., Mailer commented his decision for Texas with the following argument: "the major part of my decision (and pleasure) to have this archive go to the Ranson Center is that you have one of the best, if not, indeed, the greatest collection of literary archives to be found in America." The archive chronicling Norman Mailer's life and career from the 1930s onwards opened in 2008 (Henderson et al., 2007: 141). Consequently, Austin, Texas has became a Mailer literary destination, along with Provincetown, Massachusetts, and Brooklyn, New York, as well as the many other places around the world Mailer had visited for various reasons during his lifetime.

The legacy of Norman Mailer also continues on through the work of two non-profit organizations: the Norman Mailer Society and the Norman Mailer Center. Mailer's official biographer J. Michael Lennon, Emeritus Professor of English at Wilkes University in Texas and the custodian of Mailer's literary estate also contributes to the preservation and furtherance of Mailer's literature. Lennon maintained a close personal relationship with Mailer for more than 30 years and published widely on Mailer, including editing several of his works: *Pieces and Pontifications* (1982), *Conversations with Norman Mailer* (1988), *The Spooky Art: Some Thoughts on Writing* (2005), *On God: An Uncommon Conversation* (2007), *Norman Mailer: A Double Life* (2013), and *Selected Letters of Norman Mailer* (2014). Since Mailer never wrote his own autobiography, this 2014 book provides the readers an excellent opportunity to see into Mailer's inner life through his personal correspondence. Although the accomplished author actually did not like writing letters, he was able to dictate as many as 50 in one day. Despite thousands of letters, some lack of literary engagement in letter writing is seen in this collection. Letters are of great importance for studying Mailer's life and works, but not always of great literary value.

Selected Letters of Norman Mailer contains 714 of Mailer's letters, dating from 1940s to his death, representing less than two per cent of his entire correspondence. The Mailer archive at the Harry Ransom Center of the University of Texas at Austin, namely, contains over 1,300 cassette tapes with Mailer's dictations, each containing scores of letters. The collection includes letters to his family and friends, to fans and fellow writers (Truman Capote, James Baldwin, Philip Roth), to presidents and politicians (Bill and Hilary Clinton, Henry Kissinger, Fidel Castro etc.), to famous entertainment figures (John Lennon, Marlon Brando) and to convicted murderer Jack Abbott. These letters also provide insight into the lives of Mailer as a Harvard undergraduate, as a son, as a husband, lover, soldier, writer, political analyst, etc. The collection constitute a subtle documentary of Mailer's life (or lives) and times. According to J. Michael Lennon, Mailer demanded no changes to any of his letters, but he did make some factual corrections.

The first selected letter is from Harvard to Mailer's parents, in which he informed them that he had decided to join the literary magazine *The Harvard Advocate*. Mailer starts his letter addressing his parents as: "Dear Folks, I'm quite the busy boy now with tryouts for the *Advocate* & *Red Book*. I've dropped the *Lampoon* because 1) I can't write humorously, 2) there is $100 initiation fee." Since there are more letters to his parents in the collection, it appears that Mailer wrote to his mother and father on a regular basis.

Mailer's letters to his first wife reveal his romantic side. He starts them with "My Darling Love" and finishes: "I am amazed at how much I depend upon you. Never mind, my Beatrice, if I am cruel and jeer at your train. It soothes me and enriches me, lifts me from the slough of misery and pettiness and apathy in which I find myself always with you. /.../ I love you darling – terribly, Norman." In another letter to Beatrice, he wrote: "At the risk of being repetitive, schnoog, I want to describe another sunset to you – last nights, for it was the most beautiful one I have ever seen. It swung in the arc of the horizon from the bow all the way to starboard midships, and its curve seemed the curve of a harbor. The sun was already out of sight but its reflection did the work. The sky was very grey and heavy, and the only break of clear sky and cloud was along that particular portion of the horizon."

Since 2009, the Norman Mailer Center has awarded Mailer Prizes to great men and women of letters. The Center's website states that the Mailer Prize is awarded to those "whose work over the years has challenged readers' perspectives on the world around them" (nmcenter.org). As of 2015, the Mailer Prize has thus far been awarded to the following individuals: in 2009, Toni Morrison received the award for Lifetime Achievement, and David Halberstam for Distinguished Journalism; in 2010, Orhan Pamuk got the Mailer Prize for Lifetime Achievement, Ruth Gruber for Distinguished Journalism and Humanitarianism, and Jann Wenner for Lifetime Achievement in Magazine Publishing; in 2011, Mailer Prize recipients were Elie Wiesel for Lifetime Achievement, Arundhati Roy for Distinguished Writing, Gay Talese for Distinguished Journalism, and Keith Richards for Distinguished Biography; in 2012, the Mailer Prize recipients were Joyce Carol Oates for Lifetime Achievement, Robert A. Caro for Distinguished Biography, and Barnet Lee Rosset, Jr. for Distinguished Publishing; in 2013, the Mailer Prize recipients were Dr. Maya Angelou for Lifetime Achievement and Junot Diaz for Distinguished Writing; in 2014, the Mailer Prize recipients were Don DeLillo for Lifetime Achievement, Katrina vanden Heuvel for Distinguished Magazine Publishing, and Billy Collins for Distinguished Poetry. In 2015, Mailer Prize was awarded to Salman Rushdie for Lifetime Achievement.

5.3 Mailer – His Roots and Travels

Norman Mailer's writing career was a turbulent and exciting journey. Thus, there are many possibilities for further development of literary tourism based on the life and works of this extraordinary author. As his official biographer Michael J. Lennon points out, Mailer's literary career "had a significant foreground – in Brooklyn, Harvard, and in the Philippines – but it began officially, one might say, on one hot day in Nice" (2013: 4).

It is well known that in 1947 after finishing the manuscript of *The Naked and the Dead*, Mailer went to Europe with his wife Beatrice, and Paris was his first destination. While he was enjoying Paris and taking trips to other countries, he was trying to start a new novel (Lennon, 2013: 1). In the spring of 1948, for example, Mailer drove to Italy in a small Peugeot. He was accompanied by his wife Beatrice, younger sister Barbara and his mother Fanny. They drove from Paris east to Switzerland and then south to Italy: "It began to rain as they drove through the foothills of the Alps, and turned to snow when they reached higher elevations./.../ By the time they reached the St. Gotthard Pass, they were in a blizzard" (Lennon, ibid.). Then the group of four spent a few days in the villages and resorts of the northern lake country, and then continued their way to Florence and Venice (Lennon, 2013: 2).

Mailer's name is not connected only to the Philippines, Europe and the United Sates. Following his travels, interests and his roots, Mailer is an international author. The following are only some of the places that are related to Mailer in one way or another: Alaska (his novel *Why Are We in Vietnam?* is set in Alaska), Bellevue Hospital in New York (Mailer was committed to this hospital for psychiatric observation after stabbing his wife Adele), Boston (one of Mailer's publishers was located in Boston etc.), Brooklyn (Mailer's home was in Brooklyn above the Brooklyn Heights Promenade on Columbia Street), Berkeley (in 1972, Mailer gave a speech at Berkeley), Cannes (Mailer was a member of the jury of the 40th Cannes film festival in 1987), Switzerland (1948s and 1980s travels), Kaunas (one of Mailer's stops when travelling to Moscow in 1984), Vilnius (Mailer traveled through the city in 1984), Leningrad (Mailer visited the city of Leningrad in 1984), Chicago (Mailer covered the conventions in Chicago), Stockbridge (he bought himself and Carol Stevens a big house on Yale Hill), Mount Desert Island in Maine (the whole or the majority of the Mailer family went there each year for a month or so until 1981 when because of the bad weather the family stopped travelling to Maine and met instead in Provincetown), Mexico City (according to Mailer's daughter Susan Mailer, who lived in Mexico City, Mailer visited her a lot together with his new wife Adele, where they loved watching the bullfights), Choshi, Japan (Mailer was transferred to Japan from the Philippines while serving during WWII), Columbia University (where Mailer held a seminar for students), Cuba (where Mailer met with Fidel Castro), Dallas (Mailer visited Dallas, the scene of John F. Kennedy's assassination, on several occasions), Provincetown (where the majority of Mailer's works were written; Mailer is also buried in Provincetown), Hollywood (Mailer worked in Hollywood), England (Mailer visited England on several occasions), Lithuania (Mailer's ancestors stem from Lithuania, and according to J. M. Lennon, they lived in Panevezys, Anyksciai, and Utena), Miami (Mailer covered conventions in Miami), Philippines (Mailer was in the 112th cavalry regiment, performing various duties, including patrols), Moscow (where Mailer covered the Holyfield vs. Ibragimov fight), Minsk (visited when he was writing on Lee Harvey Oswald), Nice, Florence, Rome, and Naples (during his European travels), Paris (after WWII, Mailer studied at the Sorbonne together with his first wife Beatrice), Venice (in 1970 Mailer attended the Venice Film Festival with Carol Stevens), etc.

As far as Mailer's roots are concerned, he is partially of Lithuanian descent. According to Lennon, his grandparents lived in Lithuania, then part of Russia, and the Mailers and the Schneiders lived in three towns in Lithuania: Panevezys, Anyksciai, and Utena (2013: 7). "Unknown to each other in Russia, the two families emigrated at the end of the nineteenth century to escape economic hardship or persecution, or both, the Mailers settling in Johannesburg, South Africa, and the Schneiders in New Jersey" (Lennon, 2013: 7).

Map 1: Some of the places, cities and destinations closely connected to Mailer in the United States, Canada and Cuba.

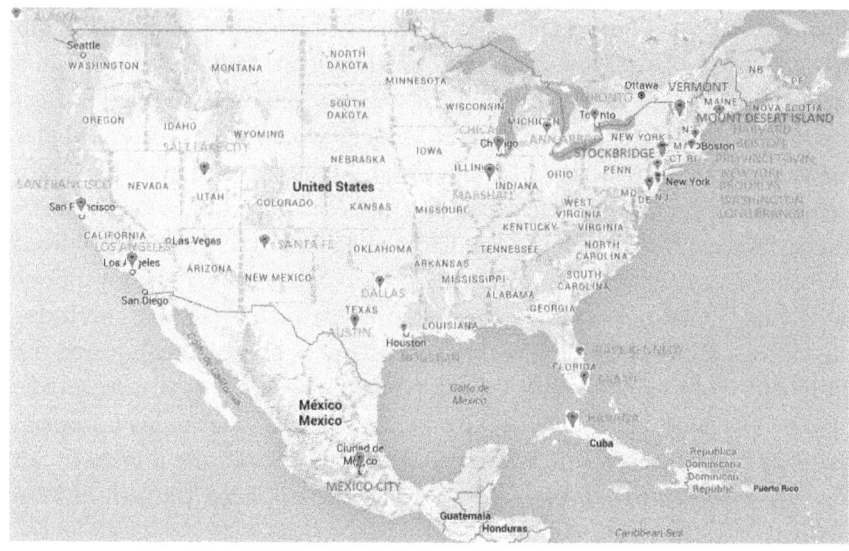

Map 2: Some of the places, cities and destinations closely connected to Mailer in Africa and Asia.

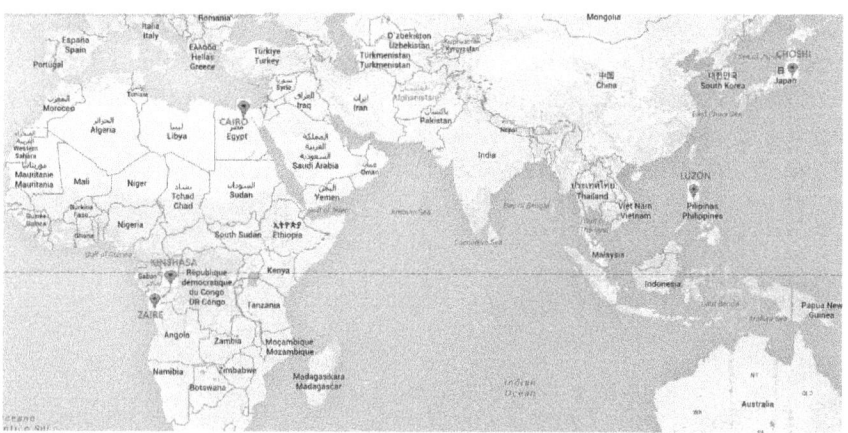

Map 3: *Some of the places, cities and destinations closely connected to Mailer in Europe and Russia.*

5.4 Brooklyn and Provincetown – Mailer's Special Literary Tourism Destinations

5.4.1 Brooklyn

Brooklyn, which is one of the five New York City boroughs (along with Manhattan, Bronx, Queens, and Staten Island) has played a significant role in American culture. The history of the city dates back to the seventeenth century, when it was founded as a Dutch settlement. Today, the city is known for many of its world-famous attractions, including the Brooklyn Bridge, the Brooklyn Museum, the Brooklyn Academy of Music, etc. And of course, there is the famous and long-standing Brooklyn literary scene, which has help make the borough a literary capital. Furthermore, "Brooklyn's bookish 'scene' has become the talk of the literary world" (Hughes, 2001: 1–2) dating all the way back to Walt Whitman, the 'grandfather' of literary Brooklyn:

> In Walt Whitman's nineteenth-century Brooklyn, we see a pastoral scene rapidly supplanted by the wild, unchecked glories and afflictions of the frantically urbanizing North and the intense polarization of the Country that led to the Civil War. In Henry Miller's reflections on his childhood, we see a jumble of European immigrant groups at the turn of the twentieth century all trying to gain a foothold on the same turf. In Hart Crane we find the fallout of the Great War giving way to 1920s prosperity and a more hopeful kind of modernity. In the narratives of Daniel Fuchs, Alfred Kazin, and Bernard Malamud, the sons of poor Jewish immigrants, we come to grips with the depths of the Depression, when families like theirs grasped at the lowest rungs of society. Thomas Wolfe, too, turned his attention to the Brooklyn streets to capture the grim 1930s /.../ William Styron's Sophie's Choice captures a postwar Brooklyn and America where new hopes commingled uneasily with the horrors of the recent past. Arthur Miller, in Death of a Salesman, gives us the archetypal faltering American businessman, unable to keep up with the postwar march of capitalism. In Norman Mailer's works, we get a close-up of U. S. soldiers in World War II; an allegory of early Cold War repression and paranoia played out in a Brooklyn boarding house; a view of the uninhibited impulses breaking out at the fringes of fifties society; an impassioned frontline report on the Vietnam protest movement /.../ (Hughes, 2011: 4–5).

Obviously, Brooklyn is a literary metropolis. It was home for a lot of famous writers, including Walt Whitman, Thomas Wolfe, Hart Crane, Truman Capote, W. H. Auden etc. (Lennon, 2013: 309–310). And it was also marked by Mailer. In terms of helping to keeping literary tourism in Manhattan alive, Mailer's Brooklyn background is very important. His Brooklyn addresses were: 555 Crown Street, 102 Pierrepont Street, 142 Columbia Heights, and 49 Remsen Street, where he wrote the classic *The Naked and the Dead*. Mailer grew up in Crown Heights. He lived elsewhere in Brooklyn Heights for much of his life, including the one-room attic studio at 20 Remsen Street (Hughes, 2011; Lennon, 214: 111). According to J. M. Lennon, the Mailers moved from Long Branch to Courtelyou Road in Flatbush, Brooklyn in 1928 (2014: 11). In 1932, they moved to 555 Crown Street in Crown Heights, where Mailer grew up "as the nice Jewish boy" (Noonan, 2013: 183).

Brooklyn, according to Noonan, is a "place of both dreams and nightmares" (2013: 176) in a symbolic sense. In *Miami and the Siege of Chicago*, Mailer says that he "was sentimental about the town" (ibid.). When he was in Chicago to report on the 1968 Democratic National Convention for *Harper's Magazine*, he wrote: "Brooklyn, however, beautiful

Brooklyn, grew beneath the skyscrapers of Manhattan, so it never became a great city, merely an asphalt herbarium for talent destined to cross the river" (72–73). Mailer believed that greatness may be achieved in Brooklyn, but to really achieve one's potential, a person should leave the borough behind. He also abandoned his Brooklyn accent and replaced it with a Cambridge elocution, which he would retain for the rest of his life (Noonan, 2013: 184). Later, Mailer returned to Brooklyn and rented a studio on 20 Ramsen Street, where he finished editing *The Naked and the Death* (Noonan, 2013: 185).

Map 4: Brooklyn, New York.

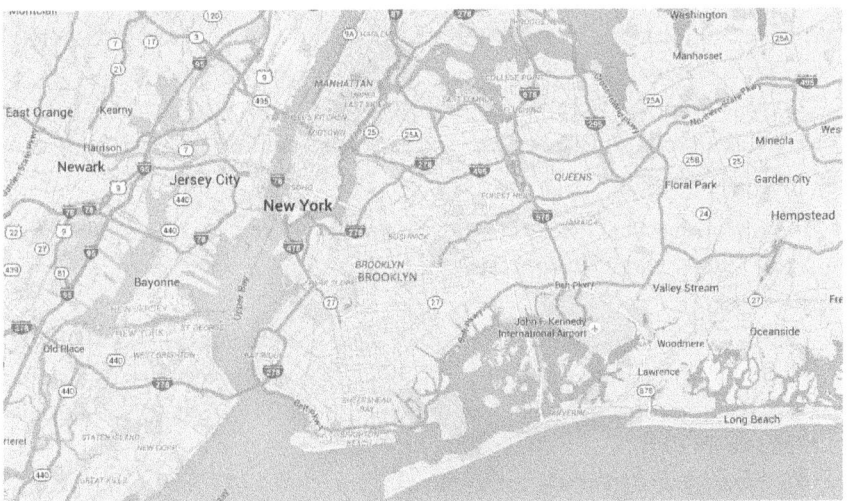

Mailer moved to 102 Pierrpont Street in Brooklyn Heights in 1943. At the time, he was 23 years old and had just returned from serving in World War II. At this address he was living with his parents until the summer, when he rented a cottage in Provincetown and began his novel *The Naked and the Dead* (Noonan, 2013: 177, Lennon, 2014: 111). At this address Arthur Miller and his wife lived below the Mailer family from 1944 to 1947 (*ibid.*).

The building at 142 Columbia Heights in Brooklyn became Mailer's home when he married Jeanne Campbell. He redesigned it to "give it the feel of a yacht." In order to get to his small writing studio eighteen feet up, "he had to climb a rope ladder and then walk across a ten-inch catwalk" (Lennon, 2013: 309–310).

When Mailer returned from Paris, he again lived at 49 Remsen for a few months before moving to Vermont and then Los Angeles, where he lived from mid-1950 to mid-1951. In 1952, Mailer (who was at the time divorced) moved to the Lower East side of Manhattan, but rented a sixth floor studio in the Ovington Building at 252 Fulton Street in Brooklyn (Lennon, 2014: 111).

For continuing Mailer's legacy, Lucas (2013) argues, the best way to promote continuing interest and debate about Mailer's work is to bring discussions about Mailer to the places where people participate (2013: 172). He also believes that interest in Mailer can be expanded by using social media, which has even become a necessity *(ibid.)*.

Today, Mailer is also a part of the Brooklyn literary tour (www.nycgo.com). Mailer buildings that can be seen on a walking tour of Brooklyn include the following:

- 142 Columbia Heights. Mailer lived here longer than in any other place. In the 1980s and 1990s, he also had a fourth floor writing studio down the street.
- 128 Willow Street. Home to Mailer's parents from 1949 until Fan's death in 1985 (Barney had died in 1972). Norris Mailer lived in a small apartment in the building before moving in with Mailer at 142 Columbia Heights in 1976.
- 102 Pierrepont Street. Home to the Mailers from 1943–1949. The American dramatist Arthur Miller lived in the same building.
- 49 Remsen Street. Norman Mailer and his first wife Beatrice lived at this address after he returned from the Second World War.
- 20 Remsen Street. Mailer wrote a large part of *The Naked and the Dead* in a one-room attic studio in this house. (Lennon 2014: 112)

5.4.2 Provincetown

Map 5: Provincetown, Massachusetts.

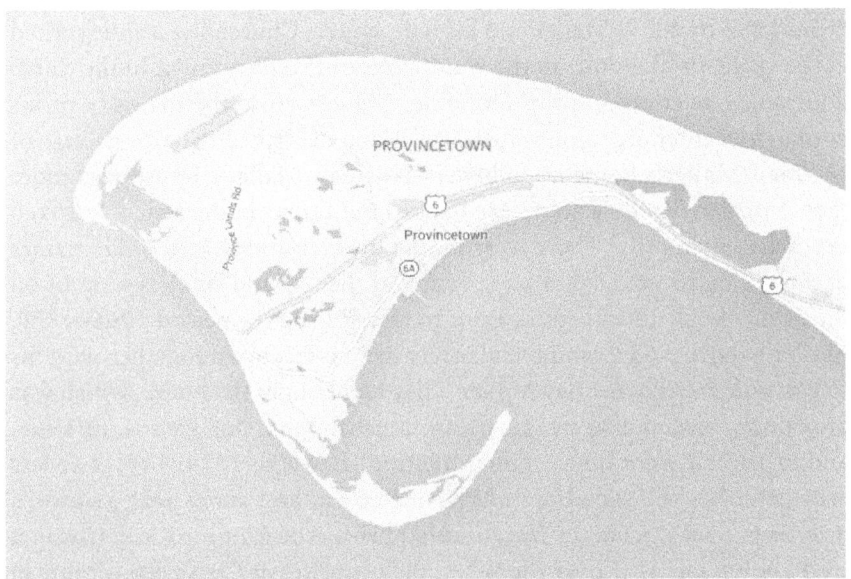

Among its other claims to fame, Provincetown is also known because of Norman Mailer, one of the town's most famous inhabitants. According to Lennon (https://medium.com/norman-mailer/norman-mailer-s-province-town), Mailer spent many summers in Provincetown, where he wrote all of his books or parts of them. Mailer's favorite journey was driving over the crest of a hill in Truro, Massachusetts, on the way to Provincetown, and first seeing "the Pilgrim Monument in all its subtle presence." Mailer believed that Provincetown was one of the most beautiful towns on the East Coast of the United States. In his 1984 novel *Tough Guys Don't Dance*, he wrote:

> *After she left, there was a week when the weather never shifted. One chill morose November sky went into another. The place turned gray before one's eyes. Back in summer, the population had beed thirty thousand and doubled on weekends. It seemed as if every vehicle on Cape Cod chose to drive down the four-lane state highway that ended at our beach. Provincetown was as colorful then as St. Tropez, and as dirty by Sunday evening as Coney Island. In the fall, however, with everyone gone, the town revealed its other presence. Now the population did not boil up daily from thirty thousand to sixty, but settled down to its honest sediment,*

> *three thousand souls, and on empty weekday afternoons you might have said the true number of inhabitants must be thirty men and women, all hiding. (Mailer, Tough Guys, 2013: 4)*

From 1982 to 2007, Mailer and his wife Norris Church lived and worked in the large, brick home on the waterfront of Provincetown. In the third-floor study overlooking the shoreline, Mailer wrote the majority of his books (nmcenter.org). Journalist Ann Wood described the atmosphere of Norman Mailer's home as follows: "Norman Mailer's house was more than Norman Mailer's home. He banged out books in the attic. He boxed in the basement. /.../ There were family dinners and heated poker games in the dining room. Drinks were drunk at the bar and smokes were lit on the deck" (wickedlocal.com). Prior to this, during the period 1966–1979, Mailer lived at 565 Commercial Street in Provincetown together with his fourth wife Beverly Bentley Mailer. They had bought the house, which was previously owned also by American novelist John Dos Passos, in 1966, and in 1979 it went up for public auction (Lawless, 2014: 118). Lawless also describes the social life of Provincetown, and states that awkward moments could occur in restaurants (116). According to her, it was a well known fact that over the years, the hostesses at Ciro's restaurants in Provincetown had to be very careful never to seat Norman next to any of his ex-wives (ibid.).

The history and cultural traditions of the town contribute to its rich heritage and thus the town is a popular tourist resort. (provincetown.com, provincetowntourismoffice.org). Mailer only added to its popularity, particularly with his novel *Tough Guys Don't Dance*, which set primarily in Provincetown. As Mailer states in *The Spooky Art* (233–34), his initial intention was also to set his 1967 novel *Why Are We in Vietnam?* in Provincetown, but he later changed his mind.

According to Mailer, Provincetown's "purpose," is to

> be the one town on the Atlantic coast that's just absolutely freer than others, where people can go and find out what they're really made of, because they can't quite find organized society agreeable enough to keep going. They want to search out the possibility of being themselves, whatever that self is.... Years ago it was bikers and guys who were really part-time criminals, drug dealers, gamblers. Then there was a period after that when the gay revolution began and then solidified in the last 10 or 15 years. So today Provincetown's a gay town, but so what?... In the next

25, 30, 40 years, it will become something else again" (quoted in Lennon, https://medium.com/norman-mailer/norman-mailer-s-provincetown-66943d75e164).

As an example of the city's commitment to freedom and civil rights, Provincetown is famous as a LGBT community and is also popular for gay marriages. May 17, 2004 was the first day when same-sex couples were legally allowed to marry in Massachusetts, making it the first American state to legalize same-sex marriage (Lawless, 133).

In Provincetown, the Norman Mailer Center organizes various events to commemorate Norman Mailer, and the Center also collaborates with the Provincetown Art Association and Museum, the Provincetown International Film Festival, the Provincetown Public Library, and other cultural and educational institutions in Provincetown and other cities, especially New York, with the goal to host events closely linked to Norman Mailer.

There is great potential for further development of literary tourism in places connected to Norman Mailer, especially by developing and presenting the numerous stories about Norman Mailer, by caring for Mailer's heritage, and also by developing tourism products based on the personality of Norman Mailer. Further on, cultural centers similar to the Norman Mailer Center could be established and filled with entertaining literary and educational programmes (e.g. discussions, workshops, conferences, festivals, etc.). By promoting Norman Mailer and his works, not only is American literature promoted, but Mailer's destinations can also be promoted and distinguished through his stories and literary works. The conceptualization of literary icons and the inclusion of their works into tourism projects, in this case the works of Norman Mailer, is significant, and perhaps not yet fully explored. In the future, Norman Mailer could be better integrated into the tourist offerings in places where Mailer lived or travelled, or his literary works touched upon. This would include many destinations, ranging from Lithuania to Provincetown.

Provincetown was also Norman Mailer's final destination. The great author is buried in the Provincetown cemetery, where his funeral took place in November 2007. On the day when Mailer was buried, his son John Buffalo read an obituary that Mailer wrote for himself, joking that by his death he had 15 divorces and 16 wives (Lawless, 149), a final piece of writing that showed Mailer's literary talent and humor until the very end.

Afterword

Norman Mailer is a twentieth-century author who had a profound impact on American literature and politics throughout the twentieth and early twenty-first centuries. Mailer reached a global audience, and his works still continue to be read around the world. This monograph provides an extensive outline of the writings of Norman (Kingsley) Mailer, which brings up new questions and answers. It is expected that Mailer will remain relevant in future intercultural dialogues, academic discourses and translation studies, and especially in American and world literatures modules, particularly given the fact that many of the themes he wrote about during his career are still relevant today (freedom, democracy, critical debate, relationships, and many more). Norman Mailer is not only a literary genius, he is one of the prominent American authors of the twentieth and twenty-first centuries. He remains one of the most controversial writers in the history of American literature, an American literary outlaw, and one of the most popular public intellectuals, who left his mark wherever he was – from Brooklyn to Provincetown.

References

"Ameriški pisatelj Norman Mailer zahteval, da na televiziji ukinejo vsa propagandna sporočila." *Slovenian Press Agency* (2005): n. pag. Web. Accessed August 12, 2010.

Begiebing, J. Robert. "Provocateur-in-Chief." *The Mailer Review* (2013): Vol. 7, No. 1. Print.

Bloom, Harold, ur. *Bloom's Modern Critical Views: Norman Mailer.* Broomall: Chelsea House Publishers, 2003.

"Bog piše boljše romane." *Delo* (1995): n. pag. Web. Accessed August 10, 2010.

Bucik, Valentin et al. "Oddelek za anglistiko in amerikanistiko." *Zbornik Filozofske fakultete Univerze v Ljubljani: 1909 – 2009.* Ljubljana: Filozofska fakulteta, 2009, 20–43. Print.

Bufithis, Philip H. *Norman Mailer.* New York: Frederick Ungar Publishing Co., 1978.

Bufithis, Philip. "*The Executioner's Song*: A Life Beneath Our Conscience." *The Mailer Review: Inaugural Issue* (2007): 77–79.

Busa, Christopher. "Why an Echo is the Shadow of a Sound: the Resonance of Metaphor in Mailer's Writing." *The Mailer Review* (2014): Vol. 8, No. 1., 317. Print.

Cobiss.net. http://www.cobiss.net. n. pag. Web. October 2015.

Collins, K. L. Ronald. "Mailer's Resistance – A Little Lesson in Free Speech." *The Mailer Review* (2014): Vol. 8, No. 1., 52–58. Print.

Connery, Thomas B. *A Sourcebook of American Literary Journalism.* Westport: Greenwood Press, 1992.

Cvijić, Anđelka. "Majlerova igra sa Đavolom." *Politika Online* (2007): n. pag. Web. Accessed August 18, 2015.

Dearborn, Mary V. *Mailer: A Biography.* New York and Boston: Houghton Mifflin Company, 1999.

Dempsey, David. 1948. "The Dusty Answer of Modern War". *New York Times. (www.nytimes.com/books/97/05/04/reviews/mailer-dead)*: n. pag. Web. December 2015.

Dickstein, Morris. 1972. "A trip to inner and outer space." *New York Times*, (January 10, 1971): n. Pag. Web. Accessed December 2015. www.graphics8.nytimes.com/packages/html/books/mailer-moon.pdf.

Dickstein, Morris. "How Mailer became, 'Mailer': the writer as private and public character". *The Mailer Review: Inaugural Issue* (2007): 118–131.

Didion, Joan. "I Want to Go Ahead and Do It.: *The Executioner's Song* by Norman Mailer." *New York Times* (October 7, 1979): n. pag. Web. Accessed December 11, 2015. www.nytimes.com/books/97/05/04/reviews/mailer-song.html.

"Dobili imperij, izgubili demokracijo." *Delo* (2003): n. pag. Web. Accessed August 10, 2010.

Edmundson, Mark. "Romantic Self-Creations: Mailer and Gilmore in *The Executioner's Song.*" *Bloom's Modern Critical Views: Norman Mailer* 2003, 127–140.

Eliot, Marc. *Song of Brooklyn: An Oral History of America's Favourite Borough*. New York: Broadway Books, Kindle Edition, 2008.

Es, Nicky van. "Literary Tourism." n. pag. Web. Accessed August 10, 2015. http://www.locatingimagination.com/literary-tourism/.

Fishkin, Shelley Fisher. *From Fact to Fiction: Journalism and Imaginative Writing in America*. New York and Oxford: Oxford University Press, 1988.

Foley, Barbara. *Telling the Truth: The Theory and Practice of Documentary Fiction*. Ithaca and London: Cornell University Press, 1986.

Glenday, K. Michael. "The Hot Breath of the Future: *The Naked and the Dead*." *Bloom's Modern Critical Views: Norman Mailer* (2003): 197–210.

Gordon, Andrew. *An American Dreamer*. Toronto: Associated University Press, 1980.

Grobel, Lawrence. *Conversations with Capote*. Boston and New York: Da Capo Press, 2000.

Gutkind, Lee. 2010. "A tribute to Norman Mailer on the 30th anniversary of the Executioner's Song's Pulitzer Prize." *Creative Nonfiction* (2010): No. 39, 6.

Hendrix, Harald. From early modern to romantic literary tourism: a diachronical perspective. In: Watson, N. J. (Ed.). *Literary Tourism and*

Nineteenth-Century Culture. Basingstoke: Palgrave Macmillan, 2009, 13–25.

Herbert, David. *Heritage, Tourism and Society*. London: Pinter, 1995.

Hughes, Evan. *Literary Brooklyn: The Writers of Brooklyn and the Story of American City Life*. New York: Holt Paperbacks, 2011.

Jurak, Dragan. "Norman Mailer: Dvorac u šumi." *Jutarnji list* (2007): n. pag. Web. AccessedAugust 11, 2015.

Kaufmann, Donald L. "*An American Dream*: The Singular Nightmare." *The Mailer Review: Inaugural Issue* (2007): 194–205.

Kernan, B. Alvin. "The Taking of the Moon: The Struggle of the Poetic and Scientific Myths in Norman Mailer's *Of a Fire on the Moon*." *Bloom's Modern Critical Views: Norman Mailer* (2003): 7–31.

Katalog knjižnica grada Zagreba. (2015): n. pag. Web. Accessed August 15, 2015. http://katalog.kgz.hr.

"Keith Richards za avtobiografijo prejel nagrado Norman Mailer." *Slovenian Press Agency* (2011): n. pag. Web. Accessed November 10, 2011.

Kazin, Alfred. "The Trouble He's Seen". *New York Times* (1968): n. pag. Web. Accessed November 10, 2015. www.nytimes.com/books/97/05/04/reviews/mailer-armies.html.

Lawless, Debra. *Provincetown Since World War II: Carnival at Land's End*. Boston: The History Press, 2014.

Leeds, Barry H. *The Enduring Vision of Norman Mailer*. Bainbridge Island: Pleasure Boat Studio, 2002.

Lennon, J. Michael, Ed. *Critical Essays on Norman Mailer*. Boston: G. K. Hall, 1986.

Lennon, J. Michael. "Why Mailer Matters." n. pag. Web. Accessed December 30, 2013. www.normanmailersociety.org/2011/12/29/ partic ipatory-journalism-of-norman-mailer.

Lennon, J. Michael. *A Double Life*. New York: Simon & Schuster, 2013.

Lennon, J. Michael, Ed. *Selected Letters of Norman Mailer*. New York: Random House: New York, 2014.

Lennon, J. Michael. "Mailer's Brooklyn." *The Mailer Review* Vol. 8, No. 1 (2014):. 111–113.

Lennon, J. Michael. Interview with Lennon on Mailer's translations by Jasna Potočnik Topler via e-mail. 2015.

Lewallen, Walter. "Back to Fort Bragg." *The Mailer Review* Vol. 8, No. 1. (2014): 319–324. Print.

Löfgren, Orvar. European Tourism In: *A Companion to the Anthropology of Europe*. Ed.: Kockel, U., Craith, M. N., and Frykman, J. Oxford: Wiley-Blackwell, 2012, 339–354.

Lucas, R. Gerald. "An Executioner for a New Age". *The Mailer Review* Vol. 7, No. 1. (2013). Print.

Lucas, R. Gerald. n. pag. Web. Accessed December 30, 2015. medium.com/@drgrlucas.

Mailer, Church Norris. *A Ticket to the Circus: A Memoir*. New York: Random House, 2010.

Mailer, Norman. *An American Dream*. New York: Dial Press, 1965.

— *Ameriški sen*. Ljubljana: Mladinska knjiga, 1966.

— *Američki san*. Zagreb: August Cesarec, 1967/1987.

— *Nepremagljivi ne plešejo*. Maribor: Založba Obzorja, 1986.

— *Advertisements for Myself*. Kindle Edition, 2013.

— *The Executioner's Song*. New York: Little, Brown & Co., 1979.

— *The Fight*. Boston: Little, Brown & Co., 1975.

— *Krvnikova pjesma*. Zagreb: Globus, 1982.

— *Krvnikova pesem*. Koper: Lipa, 1983.

— "Milosevic and Clinton." *Washington Post* (1999): n. pag. Web. Accessed August 23, 2015.

— The Armies of the Night: History as a Novel, the Novel as History. New York: The New American Library, 1968.

— *A Fire on the Moon*. London: Pan Books Ltd., 1970.

— Miami and the Siege of Chicago: An informal history of the American political conventions of 1968. Harmondsworth, Victoria: Penguin Books Ltd, 1969.

— *The Naked and the Dead*. New York: Holt, Rinehart and Winston, Inc, 1976.

— *The Spooky Art: Some Thoughts on Writing*. New York: Random House, 2003.

— *Tough Guys Don't Dance*. New York: Random House, Random House eBook Edition, 1984.

— *Why Are We in Vietnam?: A Novel.* New York: G. P. Putnam's Sons, 1967.

Mailer, Norman and M. Lennon. *On God: An Uncommon Conversation.* New York: Random House Paperback edition, 2008.

Mailer, Susan. "Master Weaver in Action." *The Mailer Review.* Vol. 8, No. 1. (2014): 52–58. Print.

Mailer Wasserman, Barbara et. al. "The Mailer Family." *The Mailer Review.* Vol. 8, No. 1. (2014): 60–61. Print.

"Malo je manjkalo, pa bi me ubil." *Delo* (1998): n. pag. Web. Accessed August 10, 2010.

Mallory, Carole. *Loving Mailer.* Beverly Hills: Phoenix Books, 2009.

Manso, Peter. *Mailer: His Life and Times.* New York: Penguin Books, 1985.

Mihovilović, Maroje. "Esej o beli možatosti razburil konservativce." *Dnevnik* (May 24, 2003). Print.

Miller, Gabriel. "A Small Trumpet of Defiance: Politics and the Buried Life in Norman Mailer's Early Fiction." *Bloom's Modern Critical Views: Norman Mailer* (2003): 67–80.

Mills, Hilary. *Mailer: A Biography.* New York: Empire Books, 1982.

Mosser, Jason. The Participatory Journalism of Michael Herr, Norman Mailer, Hunter, S. Thompson, and Joan Didion. New York: Edwin Mellen Press, 2012.

Mosser, Jason. "Norman Mailer and the Oxford English Dictionary." *The Mailer Review* Vol. 8, No. 1. (2014): 108–109.

"Nagrajen za življenjsko delo." *Delo* (2005): n. pag. Web. Accessed August 12, 2010.

Noonan, Mark. "Brooklyn Accents and the Paradox of Ambition in Norman Mailer and Arthur Miller." *The Mailer Review* Vol. 7, No. 1. (2013): 183.

"Norman Mailer odlikovan na Dunaju." *Delo* (2002): n. pag. Web. Accessed August 12, 2010.

"Norman Mailer, pisatelj: To je eden naših velikih kulturnih proizvodov: drek." *Delo* (2003): n. pag. Web. Accessed August 10, 2010.

"Norman Mailer proti Georgeu W. Bushu." *Delo* (2003): n. pag. Web. Accessed August 12, 2010.

"Normanova svetopisemska različica." *Delo* (1998): n. pag. Web. Accessed August 11, 2010.

Olster, Stacey. "Norman Mailer After Forty Years." *Bloom's Modern Critical Views: Norman Mailer* (2003): 54.

Peppard, Victor. "The Russian Reception of Norman Mailer." *The Mailer Review* Vol. 7, No. 1 (2013). Print.

Poirier, Richard. *Mailer*. Fontana: Collins Sons & Co. Ltd., 1972.

"Pokojni Norman Mailer osvojil nagrado za najslabši opis seksa." *Dnevnik* (November 29, 2007). Print.

Popov, Irena Novak. *Antologija slovenskih pesnic 1941–1980 (2nd Part)*. Ljubljana: Založba Tuma, 2005.

Potočnik Topler, Jasna. *Norman Mailer – dežurni kritik in kulturna ikona*. 1A internet: Krško 2014.

"Po 40 knjigah in 6 ženah učakal 80 let." *Slovenske novice* (January 29, 2003). Print.

"Prestiž za Normana Mailerja." *Slovenian Press Agency* (2005): n. pag. Web. Accessed August 11, 2010.

Ren, Hujun. "Norman Mailer in China: Criticism and translation." *The Mailer Review* Vol. 7, No. 1 (2013). Print.

Rhodes, D. Gary. "Norman Mailer and the Criterion Collection." *The Mailer Review* Vol. 7, No. 1 (2013). Print.

Salecl, Renata. *O tesnobi*. Ljubljana: Založba Sophia, 2007.

Smith, Joan. "Farewell to Norman Mailer, a sexist, homophobic reactionary." *The Guardian* (November 13, 2007): n. pag. Web. Accessed December 2, 2015. www.theguardian.com.

Smith, Yvonne. *Literary Tourism as a Developing Genre: South Africa's Potential*. Pretoria: University of Pretoria (dissertation). 2012.

Soban, Branko. "Zakaj je svet v vojni?" *Delo* (2004): n. pag. Web. Accessed August 10, 2010.

Squire, Shelagh. "Valuing countryside: reflections on Beatrix Potter tourism". *Area*, Vol. 25, No. 1 (1993): 1–10.

Stanonik, Janez. "The Reception of American and Canadian Literatures in Slovenia." *Cross-Cultural Studies: American, Canadian and European Literatures: 1945–1985* (1988): 329–35. Print.

Šergan, Tadeja. "Portret mladega Picassa." *Ampak* (March 1, 2005). Print.

Štefančič, Marcel. "Beli črnec." *Mladina* (2007): n. pag. Web. Accessed December 2, 2007.

Towner, John. "The grand tour: a key phase in the history of tourism". *Annals of Tourism Research* Vol. 12, No. 3 (1985): 297–333.

"Umrl dvakratni Pulitzerjev nagrajenec Norman Mailer." *Slovenian Press Agency* (2007): n. pag. Web. Accessed November 10, 2007.

"Verjamem, da hudič obstaja in deluje." *Večer* (2004): n. pag. Web. Accessed July 30, 2010.

Vince, M. Raymond. "In the Deserts of the Heart: *The Executioner's Song.*" *The Mailer Review* Vol. 8, No. 1. (2014): 291–305. Print.

"Vohuniti za samim seboj." *Delo* (1995): n. pag. Web. AccessedAugust 10, 2010.

Vrbnjak, Eva. "Per Olov Enquist." *Pogledi* (2011): n. pag. Web. Accessed August 10, 2010.

Watson, Nicola J. *The Literary Tourist: Readers and Places in Romantic & Victorian Britain*. Hampshire: Palgrave Macmillan, 2006.

Watson, Nicola J., Ed.. *Literary Tourism and Nineteenth-Century Culture*. Basingstoke: Palgrave Macmillan, 2009, 1–10.

Wenke, Joseph. *Mailer's America*. Hanover and London: University Press of New England, 1987.

Witchel, Alex. "Norris Church Mailer: The Last Wife." *The New York Times*. no pag. Web. Accessed December 20, 2015. http://www.nytimes.com/2010/04/04/magazine/04church-t.html?pagewanted=all&_r=0.

Wolfe, Tom. *The New Journalism*. London: Picador, 1996.

www.google.si/maps: n. pag. Web. Accessed November 20, 2015.

www.nmcenter.org: n. pag. Web. Accessed October 20, 2014.

www.nycgo.com: n. pag. Web. Accessed November 14, 2015.

www.provincetown.com: n. pag. Web. Accessed November 14, 2015.

www.provincetowntourismoffice.org: n. pag. Web. Accessed November 14, 2015.

www.theamericanconservative.com: n. pag. Web. Accessed September 7, 2015.

www.wickedlocal.com: n. pag. Web. Accessed November 14, 2015.

Yalkut, Carolyn. "Prophesying the News: Norman Mailer's Journalism." *The Mailer Review* Vol. 7, No. 1. (2013). Print.

Yiannakis, John N. and Amanda Davies. 2011. "Diversifying rural economies through literary tourism: a review of literary tourism in Western Australia." In: *Journal of Heritage Tourism,* n. pag. Web. Accessed November 14, 2015. DOI:10.1080/1743873X.2001.618538.

"Zadnji veliki zalet ameriške legende." *Delo* (2003): n. pag. Web. Accessed August 11, 2010.

Pictures

Map 1: Some of the places, cities and destinations closely connected to Mailer in the United States, Canada and Cuba 98

Map 2: Some of the places, cities and destinations closely connected to Mailer in Africa and Asia 98

Map 3: Some of the places, cities and destinations closely connected to Mailer in Europe and Russia 99

Map 4: Brooklyn, New York 101

Map 5: Provincetown, Massachusetts...103

Index

A
Adele 18
Adele Morales 25
Adolf Hitler 12
Adolph Hitler 75
Advertisements for Myself 25, 36, 38
Alaska 62, 96
Albania 77
America 33, 52, 67, 75, 76
American society 12, 32, 39, 41, 57, 69, 76
An American Dream 12, 26, 36, 38, 53
Ana Padovan 77
Ancient Evenings 37
anez Stanonik 80
Anopopei 39
Antonio Samons 78
Antun Šoljan 77
Anyksciai 97
Apollo 66
Apollo landing 69
Aquarius 64
ARMY 23
A Ticket to the Circus 28
A Transit to Narcissus 39
autobiography 28

B
Barbara Mailer Wasserman 17
Barbary Shore 25, 36
Beatrice 96
Beatrice Silverman 23
Bellevue Hospital 96
Berkeley 96
Beverly Bentley 26, 27, 68

Beverly Bentley Mailer 104
Bojan Rambaher 77
Boris Verbič 77
Bosnia and Herzegovina 77
Boston, 96
boxing 19
Branko Bucalo 77
Brooklyn 14, 20, 96, 100
Bulgaria 77
Bulgarian 77
bullfighting 19

C
Cannes 96
Cannibals and Christians 36
Capote 45
Carol Stevens 27
Chicago 58, 96
CHICAGO 58
children 17
Chinese 14, 77
Clas Brunius 78
Cold War 67
Crime and Punishment 44
Croatian 14, 77, 78, 80, 81, 82, 83, 84, 85, 87, 89
Cuba 97
Czech 77

D
Dallas 97
death 17
Death for the Ladies 36
death penalty 47
Deaths for the Ladies (and Other Disasters) 26
democracy 76

Dieter 75
documentary novel 34
Dotson Rader 69
Dušan Ćurčija 77

E
Emerson 44
England 97
Esquire 53
European languages 77
Existential Errands 36

F
family 17
fiction 34, 36
films 27
freedom 76
French 77

G
Gary Mark Gilmore 42
Genius and Lust 36
George Foreman 20
George W. Bush 69
German 77
Gilmore 43, 45
Gordana Bunčić 77
Greek 77

H
Harlot's Ghost 37
Harvard 22, 23, 58
Harvard University 22
Hebrew 21
Hillary Mills 17
Hitler 76
Hollywood 97
Houston 68
Hungarian 77
Hunters 62

I
Islamism 71
Italian 77
Italy 96
Ivan Slamnig 77

J
Janez Stanonik 80
Jean Malaquais 78
Jewish 20, 21
J. Michael Lennon 17, 38, 41, 125
John Buffalo Mailer 18, 37
José Manuel Calafate 78

K
Karl Marx 57
Kaunas 96
Kinshasa 20

L
Lady Jeanne Campbell 26, 53
language 33
Las Vegas 57
Latin 75
Lawrence Schiller 43
Leningrad 96
Lennon 17
Leo Strøm 78
letters 36
literary journalism 34, 35, 36
literary tourism 91, 100, 105
Lithuania 97
Lithuania, 97
Long Branch 20

M
Macedonia 77
Macedonian 14, 77, 78, 81, 85, 90
Magdalena Reljić 77
Maidstone 36

120

Mailer 11, 12, 13, 14, 17, 18, 19, 20, 21, 22, 23, 24, 25, 26, 27, 28, 29, 31, 32, 33, 34, 36, 37, 38, 39, 40, 41, 43, 44, 45, 46, 47, 49, 50, 51, 52, 53, 54, 55, 56, 57, 58, 59, 60, 61, 62, 63, 64, 65, 66, 67, 68, 69, 70, 71, 72, 73, 74, 75, 76, 77, 78, 79, 80, 81, 82, 84, 85, 86, 87, 88, 89, 90, 93, 95, 96, 97, 100, 101, 102, 103, 104, 105, 109, 110, 111, 112, 113, 114, 115
Marilyn 36, 38
Marko Maras 77
Marriage 55
married 17
Martin Luther King 59
Mary Dearborn 17
Mexico 25
Miami 58, 97
MIAMI 58
Miami and the Siege of Chicago 12, 36, 38, 73
Michael Lennon 37
Milena Benini 77
Milica Babić 77
Mills 38
Minsk 97
Mira Mihelič 77
mistresses 27
Modest Gifts 37
Montenegro 77
Moscow 97
motives 75
Muhammad Ali 20

N
Nada Ćušić 77
Naples 97
NASA 65
National Book Award 27
new journalism 34, 36

New Journalism 26
New York 17, 27, 70
New York Times 18, 24, 75
Nixon 59, 60
non-fiction 34, 36
No Percentage 39
Norman Mailer 17, 38, 61, 87, 89, 90, 93, 104, 105, 125. Glejte
Norman Mailer: A Double Life 17
Norris Church 27, 28, 104
Norwegian 77

O
Of a Fire on the Moon 12, 36
Of A Fire on the Moon 38
Of A Fire On the Moon 64, 69
Of a Small and Modest Malignancy 36
Of Women and their Elegance 36
On God 37
Oswald's Tale 37

P
Panevezys 97
Paris 96, 97
participatory journalism 47
patriotism 61
Philip H. Bufithis 17
Philippine Islands 39
Philippines 97
Phillippines 75
Phillip Sipiora 93
Pieces and Pontifications 37
Polish 77
Portrait of Picasso As a Young Man 37
Portuguese, 77
Provincetown 14, 24, 62, 68, 97, 103
Provincetown cemetery 105
Pulitzer Prize 27, 41
Pulitzer Prizes 18

R
reality 34, 35
Richard Poirier 17
Russian 14, 77, 78, 97, 114

S
Satan 68, 75
Second World War 11
September 11 70
Serbia 77
Serbian 14, 77, 78, 80, 81, 82, 83, 84, 85, 89
Slovakian 77
Slovene 77
Slovenia 77
Slovenian 14, 88, 109, 111, 114, 115
Some Honourable Men 36
space imperialism 69
Spanish, 77
Stanonik 78
Stephen Richards Rojack 53
St. George and the Godfather 36
St. Gotthard Pass 96
Stjepan A. Szabó 77
style 75
stylis 31
stylist 31
Susan Mailer 18
Swedish 77
Switzerland 96
symbolism 39
Szűr-Szabó Katalin 78

T
technology 67
television adaptation 27
terrorism 71
Texas 61
The Armies of the Night 12, 13, 27, 32, 36, 38, 49, 50, 53, 58, 80
The Big Empty 37

The Castle in the Forest 18, 37, 38, 75, 76
The Deer Park 19, 25, 36
the Democrats 58
The Executioner's Song 12, 14, 18, 27, 32, 36, 37, 38, 41, 43, 44, 45, 46, 47, 78, 80, 81, 83, 110, 112
The Fight 20, 36, 38
The Gospel According to the Son 37
The Harvard Advocate 94
The Naked and the Dead 12, 14, 24, 25, 36, 38, 39, 40, 41, 53, 70, 73, 75, 77, 78, 79, 80, 81, 85, 96, 101
The New York Times 38
The Presidential Papers 36
The Prisoner of Sex 36
the Republicans 58
The Spooky Art 37, 50
The Time of Our Time 37, 38
The Transit of Narcissus 36
The Village Voice, 17
The White Negro 36
Todor Valchev 78
Tomislav Ladan 77
Tommy Lee Jones 43
totalitarianism 60
Tough Guys don't Dance 37
Tough Guys Don't Dance 20, 27, 37, 78, 80, 81, 104
TRANSLATIONS 77

U
United States of America 12, 13, 14, 24, 33, 62, 66, 67, 72, 79, 88, 91
Utena 97

V
Venice 97

Vietnam 60, 61, 62, 63, 68
Vilnius 96
Vincenzo Mantovani 78

W
Walter Kahnert 78
Washington 47
Wenke 33
Why Are We at War? 12
Why Are We At War? 14, 37, 38, 69
Why Are We At War?. 38
Why are we in Vietnam 36

Why Are We in Vietnam? 12, 38
Why Are We In Vietnam? 61

Y
Yugoslavia 79

Z
Zagreb 79
Zaire 20
Zeitgeist 11, 32, 74
Zlatko Crnković 77
Zora 79
Zoran Mutić 77

Reviews of the Monograph

Review By Prof. Dr. Jerneja Petrič

The monograph *Literary Tourism: The Case of Norman Mailer, Mailer's Life and Legacy,* by the Slovene scholar Jasna Potočnik Topler delivers on its promise. It abounds in significant historical detail on Mailer and presents a number of important facts, many of which offer new perspectives on the legendary author. Whereas the facts are based on numerous references, Potočnik Topler's complex and thorough analysis, as well as her interpretations, offer a valuable insight into Mailer's life and sheds light upon some of Mailer's most important works and their reception in Europe. His reception in the Balkans, and a chapter on his role in literary tourism represent a most valuable addition to existing Mailer scholarship.

The monograph places a special emphasis on Mailer's works belonging to the genre of literary journalism where the role of the reader is crucial. Reading Mailer's work engages the reader in the same way this present monograph engages its reader, especially when discussing the impact of Mailer's work in the United States of America and in Europe.

Mailer's official biographer J. Michael Lennon titled his 2013 biography *Norman Mailer: A Double Life,* which inspired Potočnik Topler to title one of the chapters in her monograph "The Lives of Norman Mailer," who seems to have had a very rich life being a controversial literary and social figure, one of the most remarkable ones on the American cultural scene. The section of Potočnik Topler's monograph dealing with the reception of Mailer's work brings intriguing data on translations of his works into many languages, such as Croatian, Serbian and Slovene. It turns out that Mailer is still popular in the Balkans, or, shall we say, a novelty at least in one case: the Macedonians got their first translation of Mailer as late as 2013.

One of the highlights of this monograph is Potočnik Topler's perspective on Norman Mailer as a generator of literary tourism. She argues that many places worldwide, from Lithuania to Brooklyn, from Philippines to Paris and Provincetown, to mention just a few, were in one way or another influenced by Mailer's brilliant career. For better visualization of these locations, maps of the aforementioned places are included.

Potočnik Topler's monograph points to incredibly topical messages in Mailer's novels in which the writer draws attention to a series of highly topical issues such as careers, dehumanization, inhumanity, corruption, materialism, violence, racism, etc. The analysis of Mailer's works exposes American society as rotten and totalitarian, however, Potočnik Topler understands Mailer's criticism as his act of patriotism, as an attempt to open the eyes of fellow Americans and redirect them on the right path.

The monograph presents Norman Mailer as a literary genius who devoted his entire writing career to pointing to the wrongs of the society in order to set them straight. Even for contemporary audiences, Mailer's messages remain very topical. Due to the lack of values people all over the world are facing at least some consequences of the widespread crisis. In Mailer's work the crisis is reflected in dehumanization, materialism, violence, racism and non-human interaction.

All in all, Potočnik Topler's monograph is an intriguing read and a valuable contribution to Mailer scholarship.

Prof. Jerneja Petrič, University of Ljubljana

Review By Ddr. Natalia Kaloh Vid

This informative and insightful work Norman Mailer and his Legacy, Literary Tourism: The Case of Norman Mailer by Jasna Potočnik Topler brings out new perspectives on the life and work of Norman Mailer. From the first page of the book which is addressed to a general audience Potočnik Topler establishes a link between the areas of literature and tourism, while emphasizing the reception of Mailer in the Balkans region and translations of his works into the languages of this region. The history of translations of Mailer ranges from the 1950 and 1960s when the first translations into Serbian/Croatian and into Slovene were published until the first translations of Mailer into Macedonian in 2013. A valuable addition is also the author's critical overview of the media response on Mailer's work in the former Yugoslavia.

The monograph is divided into the following chapters: Introduction, The Lives of Norman Mailer, Mailer's Works (concentrated on The Naked and the Dead, The Executioner's Song, The Armies of the Night, An American Dream, Miami and the Siege of Chicago, Why are We in Vietnam?, Of A

Fire on the Moon, Why Are We at War, The Castle in the Forest), Mailer's Reception in Europe and in Slovenia, Mailer and Literary Tourism, which offer valuable information on Norman Mailer's life and word, while contributing to the fact that prove that Mailer's ideas are still interesting for scholars and laic readers.

The books reads quickly and is written in a catchy style. It does an excellent job exploring the most important life milestones and works by Norman Mailer. The work is undoubtedly bound to generate interest from a wide readership.

Prof. Natalia Kaloh Vid, University of Maribor

Review By Prof. Dr. Mladen Knežević

Norman Mailer is an interesting and remarkable personality in the literary and political history of the United States. And as the monograph titled *Literary Tourism: The Case of Norman Mailer, Mailer's Life and Legacy* very clearly demonstrates, this is also true for audiences outside the United States. The book represents a symbolic bridge between the American and European cultures, and the monograph demonstrates that literature is a significant tool for promoting tourism.

The five chapters of the monograph present extensive information on Norman Mailer as the literary author and activist for freedom, democracy, and human rights, thorough an analysis of the following significant works: *The Naked and the Dead, The Executioner's Song, The Armies of the Night, An American Dream, Miami and the Siege of Chicago, Why are We in Vietnam?, Of A Fire on the Moon, Why Are We at War*, and *Castle in the Forest*. This literary analysis is followed by a chapter on Mailer's reception outside the United States of America with the emphasis on his translations in the Balkans, and a chapter on Mailer's influence on literary tourism, and Mailer's enduring legacy. The latter chapters represent a significant contribution to the field of cultural studies, and especially literary tourism. The book offers insight into just how many places were important to Mailer's life, ranging from Brooklyn to the Philippines, Cuba, Alaska, Moscow, Mexico City, Kaunas, Choshi, Minsk, Paris, Cannes, and more. to Provincetown. The maps included contribute to the better presentation of the locations all over the world.

The book is a great contribution to the field of literary tourism in general, and especially in Slovenia, where literary tourism is gaining importance in tourism studies. Of particular interest is the section on Mailer's translations, because it provides the reader with the awareness of translations of Mailer's works in numerous languages, among them also languages with a small number of speakers, such as Macedonian or Slovene.

This book by Jasna Potočnik Topler brings together very diverse information on Mailer based on various references, and what is most valuable, in my opinion, is the original analysis of Mailer's works as well as the analysis of Mailer's reception in the Balkans. As it can be claimed that the Balkans has always been a special place, the book also provides us with information that Norman Mailer has always had a special place in the Balkans.

It should also be noted that the monograph by Potočnik Topler does not only reflect Mailer's work in the sense of literary history and the development of literary tourism, but it also questions modern and contemporary values.

Prof. Mladen Knežević, University of Maribor;
Editor-in-Chief of *American Journal of Tourism Management*

The value of Mailer Studies outside of the United States is undeniable. Though Mailer participated directly in American politics and culture throughout his lifetime, the central themes that run throughout his body of work transcend the concerns of just one nation. Mailer wrote extensively on issues of existential freedom, spirituality, the importance of critical thinking and debate, the dangers of conformity and totalitarianism, the complexity of gender identity, and the nature of love, all of which speak to various facets of the human condition. Thus, introducing readers in Europe and Slovenia to Mailer's work not only provides a gateway into the study of American culture and history, but also demonstrates the way literature can help to promote a global community.

Maggie McKinley, Assistant Professor of English at Harper College, Palatine, IL
Program Director of Philip Roth Society
Vice President of Norman Mailer Society

www.ingramcontent.com/pod-product-compliance
Ingram Content Group UK Ltd.
Pitfield, Milton Keynes, MK11 3LW, UK
UKHW021836210426
5322IPUK00021B/326